READINGS ON

EDGAR ALLAN POE

OTHER TITLES IN THE GREENHAVEN PRESS LITERARY COMPANION SERIES:

AMERICAN AUTHORS

Maya Angelou
Stephen Crane
Emily Dickinson
William Faulkner
F. Scott Fitzgerald
Nathaniel Hawthorne
Ernest Hemingway
Herman Melville
Arthur Miller
Eugene O'Neill
John Steinbeck
Mark Twain

BRITISH AUTHORS

Jane Austen
Joseph Conrad
Charles Dickens

WORLD AUTHORS

Fyodor Dostoyevsky
Homer
Sophocles

AMERICAN LITERATURE

The Great Gatsby
Of Mice and Men
The Scarlet Letter

BRITISH LITERATURE

Animal Farm
The Canterbury Tales
Lord of the Flies
Romeo and Juliet
Shakespeare: The Comedies
Shakespeare: The Sonnets
Shakespeare: The Tragedies
A Tale of Two Cities

WORLD LITERATURE

Diary of a Young Girl

THE GREENHAVEN PRESS
Literary Companion
TO AMERICAN AUTHORS

READINGS ON

EDGAR ALLAN POE

David Bender, *Publisher*
Bruno Leone, *Executive Editor*
Brenda Stalcup, *Managing Editor*
Bonnie Szumski, *Series Editor*

Bonnie Szumski, *Book Editor*
Carol Prime, *Assistant Editor*

Greenhaven Press, San Diego, CA

Library of Congress Cataloging-in-Publication Data

Readings on Edgar Allan Poe / Bonnie Szumski, book editor,
Carol Prime, assistant editor.
        p.   cm. — (The Greenhaven Press literary
companion to American authors)
    Includes bibliographical references and index.
    ISBN 1-56510-633-4 (lib. : alk. paper). —
ISBN 1-56510-632-6 (pbk. : alk. paper)
    1. Poe, Edgar Allan, 1809–1849—Criticism and inter-
pretation. 2. Fantastic literature, American—History and
criticism. I. Szumski, Bonnie, 1958–   . II. Prime, Carol.
III. Series.
PS2638.R43   1998
818'.309–dc21   97-12902
                                                     CIP

Every effort has been made to trace the owners of copy-
righted material. The articles in this volume may have
been edited for content, length, and/or reading level. The
titles have been changed to enhance the editorial purpose
of the Opposing Viewpoints® concept. Those interested in
locating the original source will find the complete citation
on the first page of each article.

Cover photo: UPI/Corbis-Bettmann; pages 14, 19, 24, 29:
Library of Congress

Copyright ©1998 by Greenhaven Press, Inc.
PO Box 289009
San Diego, CA 92198-9009
Printed in the U.S.A.

66*It is not in the power of any fiction to inculcate any truth.*99

———*Poe's review of Frances Osgood's play* Elfrida, *published in* Godey's Lady's Books, *August 1845*

CONTENTS

Foreword   9

Introduction   11

Edgar Allan Poe: A Biography   13

Chapter 1: Edgar Allan Poe: An Evaluation

1. An American Genius *by Charles Baudelaire*   32
Edgar Allan Poe's fascination with the macabre, his celebration of beauty and perfection, and his pursuit of dark
and difficult themes make him the most rare of American
writers.

2. Poe Is a Terrible Poet *by Aldous Huxley*   36
Poe's poetry is immature and technically poor. He overuses
rhyme, his imagery is overworked and artificial, and his
alliteration is adolescent. Poe should never be taken as a
serious poet in command of his art.

3. Poe Invented the Modern Detective Story
by Celestin Pierre Cambiaire   44
Poe's tales of ratiocination, or detective stories, were the
first of their kind. Every detective writer owes a debt to
Poe, whose Detective Dupin became a model for all later
brainy fictional sleuths.

4. Poe Heavily Influenced Other Writers
by Jeffrey Meyers   49
Poe's greatest legacy is his influence on the writers who
followed him. His pioneering work in the genres of science
fiction, mystery, horror, and detective fiction have made
him one of the most imitated writers in history.

5. Poe's Theatricality Is Essential to His Work
by W.H. Auden   57
Many critics attack Poe's work as florid and overly theatrical. But this style is essential to the mood and content of
Poe's work: By maintaining an omnipresent feeling of
doom, Poe's characters remain operatic and larger-than-
life.

6. Poe's Genius Was in Creating a Self and a Style
by N. Bryllion Fagin   64
Poe's overly dramatic life and writing style were a conscious creation. Many people have evaluated Poe as ado-

lescent in his work, almost arrested in his development. Few have seen that Poe enjoyed creating a Gothic personality, both in his life and his work.

7. Poe as Literary Critic *by Edd Winfield Parks*   75
In his own time, Poe was best known as an incisive literary critic. His work in this area heavily influenced and improved his own writing. As a critic, Poe searched for unity in the works he reviewed, and he came to want to achieve the same wholeness of purpose and brevity of style that he demanded of others.

Chapter 2 : Poe's Themes

1. Symbolism in Poe's Tales *by Georges Zayed*   82
Poe's bizarre characters and unrealistic settings are symbolic, meant to reveal unconscious truths and states of being. Poe wanted his readers to see in these exaggerated symbols the psychological truth of the human condition and our unwillingness to look at the darker side.

2. Death in Poe's Writings *by J. Gerald Kennedy*   92
Many critics have puzzled over Poe's obsession with death, which he seems to oversentimentalize and romanticize in his writings. This treatment of death did not reveal Poe's personal views, however, but was merely a convention of the time that Poe exploited to sell his work.

3. Fear as a Theme in Poe's Work
by Michael L. Burduck   101
Poe was a master of the use of fear. A good horror writer exploits people's inner fears; Poe was especially good at finding these "phobic pressure points," luring readers into his stories and terrorizing them with his spellbinding use of fear.

4. Poe's Use of Allegory *by Richard Wilbur*   110
Poe's tales are unquestionably allegorical. Every character, every setting, and every emotion is emblematic of another reality. Rather than becoming tedious, Poe's work represents allegory at its best—revealing psychological truths while maintaining an integral artistic reality.

5. Humor in Poe's Tales *by James H. Justus*   120
Many critics make the mistake of taking Poe's doom and gloom all too seriously when he is really having fun. Many of Poe's tales are quite funny, revealing a dark sense of humor that enlivens his writing.

6. Poe's Use of Horror *by Edward H. Davidson*   128
Poe used horror as a way "to externalize, in vivid physical objects, inner states of being and a method of portraying the mind's awareness of itself."

Chapter 3: A Critical Selection

1. **Poe Explains "The Raven"** *by Edgar Allan Poe* 137
   "The Raven" is a tightly constructed poem, with each line
   leading toward an inevitable conclusion. Good poetry is
   ever conscious of form, setting, and structure.

2. **"The Pit and the Pendulum": A Freudian
   Interpretation** *by Marie Bonaparte* 148
   "The Pit and the Pendulum" is a clear allegory about a
   son's fear of annihilation by his father.

3. **"Ligeia": Analyzing Poe's Love Stories**
   by D.H. Lawrence 152
   Poe's unconscious motivations to totally possess a woman
   are clearly present in his love stories. This unrealistic motivation marred his writing, as he refused in life, as in his
   art, to fully flesh out his female characters, denying them
   personalities and drives of their own.

4. **The Psychology of "The Tell-Tale Heart"**
   by E. Arthur Robinson 160
   "The Tell-Tale Heart" is a masterpiece of suspense. Poe
   achieves this spellbinding level of suspense by skillfully
   manipulating time, making seconds last like hours. The
   conflict between the two main characters is also master-
   fully handled.

5. **"The Fall of the House of Usher": An Allegory
   of the Artist** *by Daniel Hoffman* 169
   "The Fall of the House of Usher" is a skillful allegory about
   the artist and his creation. The main character's obsession
   with his sister, and his need to possess and control her, is
   meant to represent the writer and his creation.

Chronology 180

For Further Research 184

Index 187

FOREWORD

> *"'Tis the good reader that*
> *makes the good book."*
>
> Ralph Waldo Emerson

The story's bare facts are simple: The captain, an old and scarred seafarer, walks with a peg leg made of whale ivory. He relentlessly drives his crew to hunt the world's oceans for the great white whale that crippled him. After a long search, the ship encounters the whale and a fierce battle ensues. Finally the captain drives his harpoon into the whale, but the harpoon line catches the captain about the neck and drags him to his death.

A simple story, a straightforward plot—yet, since the 1851 publication of Herman Melville's *Moby-Dick*, readers and critics have found many meanings in the struggle between Captain Ahab and the whale. To some, the novel is a cautionary tale that depicts how Ahab's obsession with revenge leads to his insanity and death. Others believe that the whale represents the unknowable secrets of the universe and that Ahab is a tragic hero who dares to challenge fate by attempting to discover this knowledge. Perhaps Melville intended Ahab as a criticism of Americans' tendency to become involved in well-intentioned but irrational causes. Or did Melville model Ahab after himself, letting his fictional character express his anger at what he perceived as a cruel and distant god?

Although literary critics disagree over the meaning of *Moby-Dick*, readers do not need to choose one particular interpretation in order to gain an understanding of Melville's novel. Instead, by examining various analyses, they can gain numerous insights into the issues that lie under the surface of the basic plot. Studying the writings of literary critics can also aid readers in making their own assessments of *Moby-Dick* and other literary works and in developing analytical thinking skills.

The Greenhaven Literary Companion Series was created with these goals in mind. Designed for young adults, this unique anthology series provides an engaging and comprehensive introduction to literary analysis and criticism. The essays included in the Literary Companion Series are chosen for their accessibility to a young adult audience and are expertly edited in consideration of both the reading and comprehension levels of this audience. In addition, each essay is introduced by a concise summation that presents the contributing writer's main themes and insights. Every anthology in the Literary Companion Series contains a varied selection of critical essays that cover a wide time span and express diverse views. Wherever possible, primary sources are represented through excerpts from authors' notebooks, letters, and journals and through contemporary criticism.

Each title in the Literary Companion Series pays careful consideration to the historical context of the particular author or literary work. In-depth biographies and detailed chronologies reveal important aspects of authors' lives and emphasize the historical events and social milieu that influenced their writings. To facilitate further research, every anthology includes primary and secondary source bibliographies of articles and/or books selected for their suitability for young adults. These engaging features make the Greenhaven Literary Companion Series ideal for introducing students to literary analysis in the classroom or as a library resource for young adults researching the world's great authors and literature.

Exceptional in its focus on young adults, the Greenhaven Literary Companion Series strives to present literary criticism in a compelling and accessible format. Every title in the series is intended to spark readers' interest in leading American and world authors, to help them broaden their understanding of literature, and to encourage them to formulate their own analyses of the literary works that they read. It is the editors' hope that young adult readers will find these anthologies to be true companions in their study of literature.

INTRODUCTION

Few people will open this book without some knowledge of Edgar Allan Poe. His short stories continue to be well read at a time when many other classic authors have fallen into obscurity. He is the author of perhaps the most well remembered poem ever written, "The Raven," which lives on both in the original and in parody (even a Halloween episode of the cartoon show *The Simpsons* parodied the poem). His continued popularity among young adult readers, however, does not extend to adults, many of whom view Poe as one-dimensional. Indeed, Poe's themes and ideas do seem single-minded, as critic Lewis E. Gates notes:

> Whether the effect that Poe aims at is a shiver of surprise at the sudden ingenious resolution of a riddle, or a shudder of horror at the collapse of a haunted house, his methods of work are substantially the same, and the stuff from which he weaves his tale is equally unreal and remote from what ordinary life has to offer; it is all the product of an infinitely inventive intellect that devises and plans and adroitly arranges with an unflinching purpose to attain an effect.

Gates's analysis points out a primary truth about the majority of Poe's work, his tendency to deal with the "unreal and remote" leading to a sameness in much of his work. In story after story, poem after poem, Poe writes to achieve a single effect, a mood, drawing the reader into an intimate world of horror, death, and gruesome resurrection. His landscapes are crumbling houses, dank cellars, dark rooms, hearts pumping under floorboards—all challenging the reader to peer into the darkness to see the deeper, psychological reality that his characters and settings suggest.

Critic and scholar N. Bryllion Fagin, author of *The Histrionic Mr. Poe*, argues that Poe's true genius lies in his attempt to create this imaginative reality:

> Poe did not write stories of character, of plot, or of place: all the usual designations break down in his case. He wrote stories which attempted to transcribe the totality of a mood or

impression or feeling and to create within the reader the same totality of mood, impression, or feeling. Poe's great achievement was the creation and mastery of a method for capturing and evoking in others his special type of imaginative experience.

It is this achievement, perhaps, that keeps Poe's work in the public eye. Poe is not interested in presenting realistic characters or settings, but in achieving a reality that, for the span of the work, grips readers and holds them spellbound. Whatever the deeper meanings of much of his work, Poe is first and foremost a storyteller of the first magnitude. Whether readers enjoy his work on this level or appreciate the deeper themes addressed in many of the essays in this volume, Poe remains an essentially accessible, modern author.

Readings on Edgar Allan Poe attempts to illuminate Poe's themes and ideas in readable, intriguing essays. The book contains several helpful features for those new to literary criticism. Each essay's introduction summarizes the article's main ideas and gives a bit of background on the author. Notes explain difficult or unfamiliar words and concepts throughout the book. A chronology lists important dates in the life of the author and presents him in a broader historical context. A bibliography includes works for further research as well as historical works of interest. Finally, an annotated table of contents and thorough index make each volume in the *Literary Companion Series* a complete research tool in itself as well as a launching point for further exploration.

EDGAR ALLAN POE: A BIOGRAPHY

Edgar Allan Poe has been heralded as the founder of several literary disciplines: the short story, the detective story, even literary criticism as it is practiced today. Not only did Poe break new ground in these areas, but his critical works—on both other writers and his own writing—remain well-read pieces of good advice implemented by many writers. It is somewhat ironic, however, that Poe rarely followed his own advice, often ignoring his own precepts. He also rarely ventured outside his characteristic subject matter, plumbing the nature of death, resurrection, and the psychological horror of those obsessed with these subjects. Today, most readers of Poe outside of an appreciative critical circle think of him as a rather one-dimensional horror writer. Nevertheless, the timelessness of and attraction to Poe's work is evident in the fact that many people can still recite portions of Poe's famous poem "The Raven" and vividly remember such tales as "The Fall of the House of Usher," "The Tell-Tale Heart," and "The Cask of Amontillado."

A writer approaches the task of a biography of Poe, especially a short biography of Poe, with a great deal of caution, as both Poe and his biographers are responsible for a great deal of misinformation and exaggeration about his life. For example, immediately after Poe's death, the biographer Rufus Griswold roasted the author as a limited writer given to alcoholism, debauchery, drug addiction, and a variety of other sins. Griswold's biography remained mostly unchallenged for decades. Though later writers took issue with some of Griswold's conclusions, his life of Poe remained the accepted version. Then, in the second half of the twentieth century, a new appreciation for the works of Poe emerged. Scholars delved into Poe's correspondence, sought out and scrutinized the correspondence of others who knew Poe, and tried to ferret out the truth in the fiction about his life and works. Though much of Griswold's biography has been disproved, the basic facts of Poe's life are mired in half-truths. What continues to emerge today is Poe's role in the controversy. During his lifetime, Poe, ever eager to portray himself in the best, most aristocratic light, reinvented whole portions of his life, telling elaborate fictions about his origins and his career. N. Bryllion Fagin, author of *The Histrionic Mr. Poe,* has written that accepting Poe's tendency to reinvent his life is essential to understanding it. "For Poe, like the myth-making world, was a lusty romancer, and it is only by accepting his romancing about himself as part of the truth

Edgar Allan Poe's innovative mysteries and often morbid tales have captivated readers for more than a century.

that we can form any picture of him at all. . . . Perhaps Poe really believed, at times, that he was the grandson of Benedict Arnold, or that he had been arrested in far-off St. Petersburg." While no doubt this biography too will contain elements that fall in the realm of the challenged facts, the editor aims to record the most agreed upon elements of Poe's life and present them fairly.

Poe was born in Boston on January 19, 1809, the second son of actors Elizabeth (Eliza) and David Poe. At the time of Poe's birth, few cities could afford to sponsor a permanent theater company and actors such as Poe's parents toured from city to city. Thus Edgar's infancy was spent traveling from town to town on the East Coast. Elizabeth Poe was a talented actress capable of many demanding roles, but David Poe had only limited talent and was frequently skewered in theater reviews—sometimes the same reviews that praised Elizabeth. Despite Elizabeth's near constant employment, the Poes earned little as actors and constantly veered from one financial crisis to another. Edgar's father, disowned by his own father for taking up acting, tried to borrow money from other relatives when the family required it, but with little success. The birth of Poe's sister, Rosalie, in 1810, further strained the family's finances. While the facts surrounding the event remain obscure, most scholars believe that economic pressures coupled with his unsuccessful choice of profession led David Poe to abandon his young family sometime in 1811, virtually condemning Eliza to death.

Elizabeth attempted to continue acting to support her three children, but constant moves and grinding poverty either aggravated or contributed to her contracting tuberculosis, which worsened under the strain of her new responsibilities. Her last appearance on the stage was October 11, 1811. Shortly after, she fell desperately ill. The theater community rallied around her, giving a benefit performance to earn money for her care and posting public notices for contributions for her and the children, but Eliza died on December 8. Although Edgar Poe later claimed to not remember his mother, many scholars believe that her premature death, following the fevers, coughing of blood, hemorrhages, and pallid wasting away of tuberculosis, imprinted itself into Edgar's budding consciousness. Some scholars attribute his later fascination with the theme of young women dying tragically with this first example.

Henry Poe, Edgar's brother, went to live with David Poe's father, but because Edgar and Rosalie's maternal grandfather was himself deep in poverty, the younger orphans were not placed with relatives. Rosalie was taken into the care of William Mackenzie, a Richmond merchant, while Edgar was taken into the childless home of John and Frances Allan, also of Richmond.

After Edgar joined the Allan household, John Allan took his family to England and Scotland, where they remained for five years. The Allans were excessively proud of Edgar, who even at an early age had a talent for memorization, which the Allans encouraged by having Poe recite poems in company. While in England the Allans enrolled Poe at the age of nine in a boarding school in Stoke Newington, a small village four miles north of London. There Poe studied Latin, French, and mathematics. In an article written in 1878, scholar William Hunter describes Poe's success at the school and headmaster John Bransby's opinion of the youth:

> When he left it he was able to speak the French language, construe any easy Latin author, and was far better acquainted with history and literature than many boys of a more advanced age who had had greater advantages than he had had. I spoke to Dr. Bransby about him two or three times during my school days, having then, as now, a deep admiration for his poems. . . . In answer to my questions on one occasion, he said "Edgar Allan was a quick and clever boy and would have been a very good boy if he had not been spoilt by his parents, but they spoilt him, and allowed him an extravagant amount of pocket-money, which enabled him to get into all manner of mischief—still I liked the boy—poor fellow, his parents spoilt him!"

The Allans left England in 1820; John Allan's business was failing and Frances Allan, after having contracted tuberculosis, was becoming seriously ill. Back in Richmond, the Allans enrolled Edgar in a school run by Joseph Clarke, a classical scholar, and, later, a school run by William Burke. In Clarke's school Poe studied mathematics and read Cicero, Caesar, Virgil, Horace, and Ovid in Latin as well as Homer and Xenophon in Greek. Clarke wrote of Poe:

> He was remarkable for self-respect, without haughtiness, strictly just and correct in his demeanor with his fellow playmates, which rendered him a favorite even with those above his years. . . . As a scholar he was ambitious to excel, and tho' not conspicuously studious always acquitted himself well in his classes. His imaginative powers seemed to take prece-

dence of all his other faculties, he gave proof of this in some of his juvenile compositions addressed to his young female friends. He had a sensitive and tender heart, and would strain every nerve to oblige a friend.

In contrast to Poe's later, more melancholic bent, at Clarke's school he excelled at athletics. One of Poe's class-mates, James Preston, said that Poe "was a swift runner, a wonderful leaper, and what was more rare, a boxer with some slight training." Indeed Poe set a broad-jump record of 21 feet 6 inches.

In 1825 or 1826 Poe fell in love with and became secretly engaged to Elmira Royster, the fifteen-year-old daughter of his neighbor. Around this time Poe became estranged from John Allan. Poe's continued interest in poetry and romantic pursuits severely clashed with Allan's practical nature. And Poe's melancholy seems to have irritated Allan. In a letter written to Edgar's older brother, Henry, on November 1, 1824, Allan expresses some of the same sort of dismay that parents of teenagers today might voice.

> [Edgar] has had little else to do for me, he does nothing & seems quite miserable, sulky & ill-tempered to all the Fam-ily. How we have acted to produce this is beyond my concep-tion—why I have put up so long with his conduct is a little less wonderful. The boy possesses not a Spark of affection for us, not a particle of gratitude for all my care and kindness to-wards him. I have given him a much superior Education than ever I received myself.

In 1826 Poe enrolled at the University of Virginia in Char-lottesville. (It is interesting to note that Poe attended the uni-versity while its founder, Thomas Jefferson, was still in-volved with the institution. Every week, Jefferson invited a few students to Monticello to dine with him.) Poe's years at the university have been scrutinized by scholars, since it is during these years that Poe and Allan became estranged. Though Poe excelled academically at the university, finan-cially he got into disastrous trouble. Most scholars seem to agree that Allan did not give Poe sufficient funds to support himself at the university. Poe resorted to gambling to pay his debts, and whether the product of unscrupulous cheating or of his own bad luck, Poe was soon so deeply in debt that he had no hope of repaying without Allan's help. Allan, how-ever, was not inclined to pay the debts and was infuriated by Poe's attempt to blame Allan for his insufficient funds. No longer able to pay for his education, his funds cut off by his foster father, Poe was forced to leave the university in December 1826.

Back in Richmond, Allan put Poe to work at his counting-house without pay. While engaged in this profession for which he had neither talent nor enthusiasm, Poe learned that Elmira Royster had become engaged to another man. Elmira's father had been intercepting Poe's correspondence to her, and Elmira, thinking herself abandoned by Poe, accepted the proposal of Alexander Shelton.

Suffering from the combined disappointments of leaving the university, working at the countinghouse, and losing his fiancée, Poe decided to leave Richmond for Boston in 1827. An aggrieved Poe wrote to Allan:

> My determination is at length taken—to leave your house and endeavor to find some place in this wide world, where I will be treated—not as *you* have treated me. . . .
>
> Since I have been able to think on any subject, my thoughts have aspired and have been taught by *you* to aspire, to eminence in public life—this cannot be attained without a good Education. . . .
>
> [I hope] to place myself in some situation where I may not only obtain a livelihood, but lay by a sum which one day or another will support me at the University.

Then, after berating Allan, Poe had the nerve to ask him for funds to leave. The shameless request would become a pattern with Poe, who never seemed to learn that this combination of scolding and pleading for money did nothing to endear him to Allan, who became increasingly frustrated and angry with Poe for his ingratitude.

From this moment on, Poe would never recover a stable life. Critic Edward Davidson sums up Poe's tragic existence this way:

> Part of Poe's personal tragedy was that he was carefully reared through the first eighteen years of his life to conform to the manners and code of the aristocratic, landed gentry in the fashionable circles of sophisticated Richmond; then he was suddenly thrust into the business world where the only money he ever made came from that otherwise discredited instrument in the world of finance—a writer's pen.

Unable to find work for six weeks after arriving in Boston, Poe enlisted as a common soldier in the U.S. Army under the name of Edgar A. Perry. During this period, Poe paid to have his first book published. Entitled *Tamerlane and Other*

After being expelled from West Point, Poe moved in with his widowed aunt, Maria Clemm (pictured), and her young daughter, Virginia.

Poems, it appeared without his name, the only attribution being "By a Bostonian."

Because of his superior education, in the army Poe was given a post as clerk, taking dictation from officers, preparing the payroll, and acting as a messenger. Although quickly disenchanted with the army and soon desperate to leave, Poe was a success there. In nineteen months he attained the highest enlisted rank. Nevertheless, unhappy because his lack of social standing prevented him from rising to the rank of officer, Poe decided to seek officer's rank by applying to West Point. He paid a man twenty-five dollars of a promised seventy-five dollars to take his place in the army (a necessity at the time if one wished to leave the military earlier than the promised five-year stint) and was discharged in April 1829.

A couple of months before his discharge, Poe had been able to forge a tentative reconciliation with his foster father after the death of his foster mother, Frances, in February 1829. On temporary leave in March, Poe and Allan found common ground in their grief. The reconciliation would not last, however, as Poe continued to dun Allan for money and Allan resolutely continued to refuse, trying to force Poe to become more self-supporting.

Meanwhile, Poe solicited letters of recommendation to West Point from friends and finally entered the academy in 1830. He continued to pursue his literary ambitions, as well, having obtained a publisher for his second book of poetry, *Al Aaraaf, Tamerlane and Minor Poems*, in 1829. Although this second volume, published in an edition of 250, gained slightly more critical notice than his first, it, too, failed to make the impact Poe desired.

Poe quickly found that West Point was not for him, either. He balked at the rigors of the academy and almost immediately began pleading with Allan for permission to resign. Increasingly despondent, Poe turned once again to gambling and drinking for solace. When Allan refused to give permission for a resignation, Poe decided on a less honorable way to escape West Point by getting himself court-martialed. In January 1831 Poe disobeyed orders, failed to show up for roll call and guard duty, and generally violated enough rules to be tried for and convicted of gross neglect of duty and disobedience of orders. On March 6 Poe was dismissed.

As usual, Poe wrote Allan, blaming him for his fate at West Point and renewing his plea for money. Allan, who had remarried, and who would eventually have three children with his second wife as well as illegitimate twins with his mistress, was even less inclined to listen to Poe's pleas. With any hope of inheritance almost completely obliterated, Poe's continued self-pitying pleas further wearied Allan, who severed their relationship.

Now entirely on his own, Poe left for New York and then Baltimore, eventually settling with his biological father's widowed sister, Maria Clemm, and his nine-year-old cousin, Virginia, in May 1831. The Clemms lived on the edge of poverty, Maria supporting herself and her daughter by sewing and keeping boarders, aided by a pension to her bedridden mother, Elizabeth. While living with Maria, Poe renewed his relationship with his elder brother, Henry, who had been reared by Elizabeth and her husband. When Henry died of tuberculosis in 1831 at twenty-four, Poe took on his role as the man of the Clemm household.

During his years with the Clemms in Baltimore, Poe published five stories in the *Philadelphia Saturday Courier:* "Metzengerstein," "The Duc de l'Omelette," "A Tale of Jerusalem," "Bon Bon," and "Loss of Breath." Poe also won a literary contest sponsored by the Baltimore *Saturday Visiter* with "MS. Found in a Bottle." The small amount of money that Poe brought in from writing could not lift his newfound family out of poverty and Poe again attempted a reconciliation with his foster father. Hearing that Allan was ill, Poe returned to Richmond on February 14, 1834. Instead of welcoming the prodigal son, however, Allan is said to have raised his cane, threatened him, and ordered him out. His father died six weeks later.

Ever in need of employment, especially after the death of Elizabeth Poe and the loss of her pension, Poe was able to attain with the help of friends the editorship of the *Southern Literary Messenger* in Richmond. Though extremely adept at his task, Poe missed Maria and Virginia, still in Baltimore. He began to drink heavily and experience violent mood swings; his exasperated publisher Thomas Willis White sacked him.

The unemployed Poe returned to Baltimore and convinced the Clemms to join him in Richmond. Writing to White with promises to reform, Poe convinced White to reinstate him in December 1835. While at the *Messenger,* Poe became known for his scathing reviews of books, which provoked criticism from writers at other journals but were popular with Poe's readers. Poe also used the *Messenger* as a venue for his own work, including his seven *Tales of the Folio Club,* as well as "Berenice," "Morella," and "The Unparalleled Adventure of One Hans Pfaall."

While continuing to publish stories, Poe became tremendously productive at the *Messenger,* the stability of his home life contributing to his ability to work. He also devoted much of his time to educating Virginia Clemm, for whom at some point he began to feel more than brotherly love. On May 16, 1836, the twenty-seven-year-old Poe publically married the fourteen-year-old Virginia. (He had actually married her at thirteen in a private ceremony a year earlier.) The marriage did little to improve Poe's spirits, however, as he continued to suffer from bouts of depression brought on by his drinking. Many scholars, including biographer Jeffrey Meyer, are convinced that Poe suffered from either an allergy or an extreme sensitivity to alcohol that made him irascible even after a single drink. Meyers, who believes Poe inherited his alcoholism from his father, describes Poe's alcoholism this way:

> The origins of Poe's alcoholism go back to his infancy, when his nurse tranquilized him with bread soaked in gin, and to his childhood, when he toasted the dinner guests. . . . At the university he compulsively gulped down alcohol during his drinking bouts at West Point. . . . Though Poe needed no excuse to start drinking, he sought relief in alcoholic binges during times of emotional stress. He drank when he was in danger of losing Virginia, after her first hemorrhage and after her death. He drank when overwhelmed by work and by poverty. . . . He drank to calm his nerves. . . . He drank before and after his public lectures in New York and Boston, incapacitating himself for the former and disgracing himself after the latter.

Poe's continued drinking frustrated White, publisher of the *Messenger*. Though Poe had made significant contributions to the journal, perhaps singlehandedly increasing its circulation from five hundred to thirty-five hundred, White again reached the point of firing him:

> Highly as I really think of Mr. Poe's talents, I shall be forced to give him notice . . . that I can no longer recognize him as editor of my *Messenger*. Three months ago I felt it my duty to give him a similar notice—and was afterwards overpersuaded to restore him to his situation on certain conditions—which conditions he has again forfeited. Added to all this, I am cramped by him in the exercise of my own judgment, as to what articles I shall or shall not admit into my work. . . . I mean to dispense with Mr. Poe as my editor.

Thus, in January 1837 Poe left the *Messenger*.

After losing his job, Poe, Virginia, and Maria moved to New York, where they continued to live in poverty, but Poe cut back on his drinking. New York's high cost of living prompted a move to Philadelphia in the summer of 1838, where they acquired a black cat called Catterina who might have been the inspiration for Poe's story "The Black Cat." Poe continued to publish and work on *The Narrative of Arthur Gordon Pym*, two installments of which he had published while editor of the *Messenger*. *Pym* is a full-length novel depicting a supposed true-to-life adventure. Poe also published "Ligeia" in 1838.

In May 1839 Poe obtained an editorial position with *Burton's Gentleman's Magazine*. William Burton, owner of the magazine, and Poe began to clash almost immediately, mostly over Poe's caustic literary critiques. Burton wanted Poe to tone down the pieces. Poe replied, "You see I speak plainly, I cannot do otherwise upon such a subject." Despite such disagreements, Poe continued as assistant editor, and, as was his custom, used the magazine as a venue for publishing his stories. He published "The Man That Was Used Up," and his most well known work, "The Fall of the House of Usher," in September 1839. The popularity of "Usher" brought Poe to the attention of the publisher Lea and Blanchard, who agreed to publish *Tales of the Grotesque and Arabesque*, a collection of twenty-five stories in two volumes.

The book received mixed reviews. While the *Boston Notion* said that the tales "fall below the average of newspaper trash," the *Philadelphia Saturday Courier* proclaimed the tales "wildly imaginative in plot; fanciful in description . . . possessed of rare and varied learning." Despite the attention, the book sold poorly.

In May 1840 Burton put his magazine up for sale and fired Poe, in part because of their many disagreements and in part because of Poe's drinking. Poe tried to find subscribers to launch his own magazine, the *Penn*, without success. The new owner of *Burton's*, George Graham, started a magazine called *Graham's*, hiring Poe as editor for eight hundred dollars a year. Under Poe's guidance, including his continued reviews and tales, *Graham's* prospered. In just over two years, subscriptions rose from twenty-five thousand to forty thousand. Unfortunately, Poe's salary remained the same.

Poe enlivened *Graham's* with a number of innovative ideas, including a running cipher contest in which he boasted of being able to solve any puzzle the subscribers came up with. Unfortunately, the popularity of the column left Poe with little time for anything besides solving the puzzles. He disbanded the column. Poe published some of his best stories in *Graham's*, including "The Murders in the Rue Morgue," which debuted Poe's inventive detective Auguste Dupin, in April 1841. Auguste Dupin remains one of the most original and well-remembered characters in literature. "Descent into the Maelstrom" was also published at this time.

In spite of his stable position, Poe's financial circumstances remained precarious. Although the inventive Maria Clemm managed to keep her family barely fed on Poe's salary, they were never able to afford adequate food nor pay for warm lodgings. Under these conditions, Virginia, who had contracted tuberculosis, worsened. While singing and playing the piano in January 1842, she began hemorrhaging from a broken blood vessel. Although Virginia's condition would alternately improve and worsen over the next few years, she would never fully regain her health. Poe's response to her illness was an almost obsessive fear of losing her.

The year 1842 was memorable for Poe because he met two literary giants of his time, Charles Dickens and Nathaniel Hawthorne. In fact, Dickens offered to help Poe

As a result of their poor living conditions, Virginia Clemm Poe contracted tuberculosis—the same disease that had killed Poe's mother.

find an English publisher for his works. Although the effort proved unsuccessful, they remained acquaintances throughout Poe's life. Poe corresponded with Hawthorne after he reviewed several of his works in *Graham's*, including *Twice-Told Tales* and *Mosses from an Old Manse* in November 1847. Poe's reviews of Hawthorne's work were always mixed; in his review of *Mosses from an Old Manse*, Poe praised Hawthorne's writing but condemned him for overworking his allegory. Hawthorne responded to Poe's criticism with a letter urging him to return to writing his own tales:

> I admire you rather as a writer of tales than as a critic upon them. I might often—and often do—dissent from your opinions in the latter capacity, but could never fail to recognize your force and originality in the former.

The years 1842–1843 were marked by the publication of some of Poe's best-known stories, including "The Masque of the Red Death," "The Mystery of Marie Roget," "The Gold-Bug," "The Black Cat," and "The Tell-Tale Heart." Poe continued to earn little more than his salary at *Graham's*, however, which, because of Virginia's medical expenses, was woefully inadequate to support the Poe family. Poe resorted to hack writing to supplement his income.

In April 1842 Poe resigned from *Graham's* with a combination of complaints, including "disgust with the namby-pamby character of the Magazine—a character which it was impossible to eradicate.... The salary, moreover, did not pay me for the labor I was forced to bestow." Falling into the despair that plagued him all his life, Poe returned to drinking heavily after his resignation.

In 1843 Poe tried lecturing for fees. An effective speaker, Poe lectured on and recited American poetry and gave a scathing critique of Rufus Griswold's volume *The Poets and Poetry of America*. His lectures proved successful, always delivered to sold-out audiences.

In April 1844 Poe left Philadelphia for New York and another crack at the city that was even then known as a literary and publishing mecca. Poe began writing for the New York *Evening Mirror*, and was appointed its editor in the same year for $750 a year. Poe continued to publish his own pieces, including his poem, "Dream-land" in *Graham's* and four stories in other popular journals, "A Tale of the Ragged Mountains," "The Balloon-Hoax," "The Purloined Letter," which featured Dupin, and "The Premature Burial."

"The Balloon-Hoax," the tale of a magnificent balloon adventure that becomes an outer-space excursion, published in the New York *Sun,* was a sensation on the scale of "The War of the Worlds" radio broadcast over a century later. Poe's description of the public's response:

> On the morning of its announcement, the whole square surrounding the *Sun* building was literally besieged, blocked up. . . . I never witnessed more intense excitement to get possession of a newspaper. As soon as the first few copies made their way into the streets, they were bought up, at almost any price, from the news-boys, who made a profitable speculation.

In November 1845, Poe published his most famous poem, "The Raven." Poe himself felt that he had achieved something wonderful with the poem, proclaiming to friends that he had authored "the greatest poem ever written." Published in magazines throughout the country, "The Raven" made Poe a celebrity, and he was invited to salons throughout New York. In February 1845 Poe's popularity was enhanced when poet James Russell Lowell made Poe the subject of a biographical essay in *Graham's.*

In February 1845 Poe became coeditor of the *Broadway Journal* and was offered one-third of the magazine's profits. Poe reviewed many well-known classic and contemporary authors for the magazine , including Milton, Burns, Lamb, Leigh Hunt, Shelley, Tennyson, and Lowell.

Poe's fame after publication of "The Raven" brought him into contact with poets of the day, including several well-known women poets. Poe struck up a romantic mutual admiration society with one of these poets, Frances (Fanny) Sargent Osgood, in 1845.

Capitalizing on Poe's popularity, Wiley and Putnam published twelve of Poe's stories in the collection *Tales. Tales* was praised in reviews in both America and England and Wiley and Putnam followed its success with a book of Poe's poetry, *The Raven and Other Poems,* in November 1845.

Meanwhile, Poe had gone back to his old habits during his editorship at the *Broadway Journal,* alternately drinking and falling into bouts of irrationality. While coeditor Charles Briggs sought to fire Poe, the financially teetering journal collapsed, and publisher John Bisco sold it to Poe for fifty dollars. Poe unsuccessfully and feverishly sought investors for the magazine; he veered on the edge of a nervous breakdown, writing, "[I am] dreadfully sick and depressed . . . I seem to have just awakened from some horrible dream, in which all was confusion and suffering. . . . I really believe that I have been mad."

Part ownership of a journal, the publication of "The Raven," and the popularity of *Tales* and *The Raven and Other Poems* should have brought Poe some financial and professional stability; he instead fell into drunken despair and even deeper poverty than ever before.

In November 1846 Poe published "The Cask of Amontillado" in *Godey's Lady's Book*. Virginia's health continued to decline; she suffered, as Meyers explains in his biography of Poe, "irregular appetite, facial pallor, flushed cheeks, unstable pulse, night sweats, high fever, sudden chills, shortness of breath, chest pains, severe coughing and spitting of blood. Each day, as the microscopic organisms gnawed through her tissue and destroyed a bit more of her lung, she found it increasingly difficult to breathe."

With the onset of winter, lacking blankets, food, and heat, Virginia worsened alarmingly; on January 30, 1847, she died at the age of twenty-four, at the same age and of the same disease as Poe's mother. Poe promptly fell into a deep depression and drank heavily.

> I became insane, with long intervals of horrible sanity. During these fits of absolute unconsciousness I drank, God only knows how often or how much. As a matter of course my enemies referred the insanity to the drink rather than the drink to the insanity.

Poe turned for solace, and even romantic attachment, to Fanny Osgood, who remained, as she had been since meeting Poe, separated from her husband. Although Fanny seems to have enjoyed the relationship, she refused Poe's pleas to marry him.

Poe continued to sink more deeply into poverty and despair, but managed to write and publish "Ulalume," his classic poem written in imitation of ululation, or wailing, in December 1847. He also completed the almost incomprehensible philosophical work *Eureka*. Before seeking its publication, Poe promoted the work in a series of lectures, where his ideas were unevenly received. Despite the lukewarm response, Poe managed to convince George Putnam to publish *Eureka*. Putnam recalled the meeting:

> A gentleman with a somewhat nervous and excited manner claimed attention on a subject which he said was of the high-

est importance. Seated at my desk, and looking at me a full minute with his "glittering eye," he at length said: "I am Mr. Poe.". . . After another pause, the poet seeming to be in a tremor of excitement, he at length went on to say that the publication he had to propose was of momentous interest.

Poe grandiosely envisioned an edition of fifty thousand copies; Putnam wisely brought it out at five hundred—and had a difficult time selling those.

Poe felt unhinged by Virginia's death. He sought to replace her as soon as possible by remarrying, and simultaneously sought the affections of three women—Marie Louise Shew, Annie Richmond, and Sarah Helen Whitman. None of these love interests, except for the remote possibility of Sarah Helen Whitman, was destined to succeed. Marie Louise Shew, the intensely religious nurse to Poe and Virginia, was persuaded by her pastor that the man who had written such a secular book as *Eureka* was neither a suitable mate nor friend. Annie Richmond, though friendly with Poe, was a married housewife with four children. Sarah Helen Whitman, a poet herself, at one point accepted Poe but wisely realized that Poe's erratic behavior was a warning. His zealous attempts to find a wife seem not to have dampened his poetic tendencies, however, as during this period Poe wrote "The Bells" and a second "To Helen." He also completed his well-known essay on poetry, "The Poetic Principle."

In 1849, his attempts at remarriage a shambles, Poe managed to publish "Hop-Frog," "Melonta Tauta," "Von Kempelen and His Discovery," and the poems "Eldorado," "To My Mother," and "For Annie."

In this last year of his life Poe was tremendously restless, shuttling between New York, Philadelphia, Virginia, and Maryland. The rush of events that led up to Poe's death have remained mysterious. On June 29 Poe left New York for a lecture tour in an attempt to earn money to launch his own magazine, which he had named the *Stylus*. The next day, on a stop in Philadelphia, he began to drink and was arrested for public drunkenness. At some point, Poe lost his suitcase. While jailed, Poe began to hallucinate; his frightening visions included Maria Clemm being butchered.

Released from jail, Poe tried to return to New York, but, still delusional, he thought that two men on the train were plotting to kill him and he disembarked, returning to Philadelphia. He stayed with John Sartain, an artist who had

Poe's residence at the time of his death. He died in a Baltimore hospital on October 7, 1849.

worked with Poe at *Burton's* and had remained a friend. Beginning to recover, Poe located his missing suitcase at the train station on July 10. With borrowed money, Poe was able to get to Richmond for lectures on "The Poetic Principle" on August 17 and September 24 and Norfolk on September 14. While in Richmond, Poe renewed his acquaintance with his childhood love, Elmira Royster Shelton, who had been widowed for five years. Seeing opportunity, Poe tried but failed to convince her to marry him.

On September 27 Poe began the return trip to New York. He stopped in Baltimore, began to drink heavily, and again suffered from hallucinations. No one really knows what happened between September 28 and October 3, when Poe was found semiconscious and apparently desperately ill outside Gunner's Hall, an Irish tavern. The man who found him sent a note to Poe's friend Joseph Snodgrass, describing Poe's condition.

Snodgrass was appalled by what he saw. He believed that the ragged clothes Poe was found in were not his own:

> His hat—or rather the hat of somebody else, for he had evidently been robbed of his clothing, or cheated in an exchange—was a cheap palm-leaf one, without a band, and soiled; his coat, of commonest alpaca, and evidently "secondhand"; his pants of gray-mixed cassimere, dingy and badly

fitting. He wore neither vest nor neckcloth, if I remember aright, while his shirt was sadly crumpled and soiled.

Snodgrass further noted that Poe's

> face was haggard, not to say bloated, and unwashed, his hair unkempt, and his whole physique repulsive: The intellectual flash of his eye had vanished, or rather had been quenched in the bowl.... He was so utterly stupefied with liquor that I thought it best not to seek recognition or conversation.... So insensible was he, that we had to carry him to the carriage as if a corpse. The muscles of articulation seemed paralyzed to speechlessness, and mere incoherent mutterings were all that were heard.

Snodgrass put Poe in Washington College Hospital, where he lingered unconscious for ten hours. He then regained consciousness but was hallucinating and delirious. There was little that could be done for him; Poe died on October 7 and was buried in the Presbyterian Cemetery in Baltimore on October 8. Maria Clemm, who had not seen Poe since June 29, was not notified of Poe's death or funeral.

Various causes of Poe's death have been advanced, including brain fever, brain tumor, meningitis, epilepsy, syphilis, hypoglycemia, and, most recently in 1996, rabies. R. Michael Benitez, assistant professor of medicine at the University of Maryland Medical Center, believes that Poe's symptoms describe a near classic case of rabies. Details such as Poe's refusal to take anything to drink, Benitez argues, may have meant he had difficulty swallowing, a symptom of rabies. The delirium tremens, perspiration, hallucinations, and shouting at imaginary companions are also typical symptoms of end-stage rabies, in which the patient, growing increasingly confused and belligerent, finally dies. Benitez analyzed Poe's case for a clinical conference as an exercise in diagnosing the illness of a hypothetical patient. Although an interesting theory, so many years after his death it is necessarily speculation, and Poe's end remains impossible to explain with certainty.

Immediately after Poe's death, Rufus Griswold, Poe's literary executor and editor, published an obituary in which he intoned that Poe was a literary hack and hopeless drunk who had no friends. Griswold, perhaps harboring vengeful feelings because Poe had attacked him in print, began an immediate assault on Poe's character. Thus began the myths surrounding Poe's life which bring us full circle in this biography.

CHAPTER 1

Edgar Allan Poe: An Evaluation

READINGS ON
EDGAR ALLAN POE

An American Genius

Charles Baudelaire

French poet Charles Baudelaire translated Poe's tales
into French and wrote introductions to French
editions of Poe's works, as well as several long essays
championing Poe. Baudelaire was responsible for
popularizing Poe in France, claiming to see the same
themes that can be found in his own work, including
the idea of the alienated artist rebelling against society.

I have little to say about the works of this singular genius; the
public will show by its response what it thinks of them. It
would be difficult for me, perhaps, but not impossible, to un-
ravel his method, to explain his technique, especially in that
part of his works whose principal effect lies in a well-
handled analysis. I could introduce the reader to the mysteries of his workmanship, speak at length about that aspect of
American genius which makes him delight in a difficulty
overcome, an enigma explained, a successful tour de force—
which impels him to play, with a childish and almost perverse pleasure, in a world of probabilities and conjectures,
and to create the *hoaxes* which his subtle art has made seem
plausible. No one will deny that Poe is a marvelous trickster
and yet I know that he attached the greatest value to another
aspect of his work. I have some more important, though
brief, remarks to make.

It is not by these material miracles, which nevertheless
have made his reputation, that he will win the admiration of
thinking people, it is by his love of the Beautiful, by his
knowledge of the harmonic conditions of beauty, by his profound and plaintive poetry, carefully worked, correct and as
transparent as a crystal jewel—by his admirable style, pure
and bizarre—as closely woven as the mesh of armour—com-
plaisant and meticulous, whose slightest intention serves to
lead the reader gently toward the desired effect—finally and
above all by his very special genius, by that unique tempera-

Excerpted from the Preface to Charles Baudelaire's *Histoires Extraordinaires*, 1856.
Translated by Joan F. Mele in *Fatal Destinies: The Edgar Poe Essays* by Charles Baudelaire (Woodhaven, NY: Cross Country Press, 1981). Copyright ©1981 by Joan F. Mele.

ment which allowed him to paint and to explain, in an impeccable, gripping and terrible manner, the *exception in the moral order.* Diderot,[1] to take one example among a hundred, is a sanguine author; Poe is a writer who is all nerves, and even something more—and the best one I know.

In his case every introductory passage quietly draws you in like a whirlpool. His solemnity takes the reader by surprise and keeps his mind on the alert. Immediately he feels that something serious is involved. And slowly, little by little, a story unfolds in which all interest depends on an imperceptible intellectual deviation on a bold hypothesis, on an imprudent dose of Nature in the amalgam of faculties. The reader, seized by a kind of vertigo, is constrained to follow the author through his compelling deductions.

POE'S ABILITY TO UNNERVE READERS

No man, I repeat, has told about the *exceptions* in human life and in nature with more magic—the enthusiastic curiosities of convalescence, the dying seasons charged with enervating splendors, hot, humid and misty weather when the south wind softens and relaxes one's nerves like the strings of an instrument, when one's eyes fill with tears which do not come from the heart—hallucinations first seeming doubtful, then as convincing and as rational as a book—the absurd establishing itself in one's mind and controlling it with a frightful logic—hysteria usurping the place of the will, contradiction set up between the nerves and the mind, and personality so dissonant that it expresses sorrow with laughter. He analyzes whatever is most fleeting, he weighs the imponderable and describes in a meticulous and scientific manner, the effects of which are terrible, all that imaginary world which floats around a very nervous man and leads him into evil.

The very fervor with which he throws himself into the grotesque out of love for the grotesque and into the horrible out of love for the horrible serves to verify the sincerity of his work and the harmony between the man and the poet.—I have already pointed out that, in several men, this fervor was often the result of a very great unused vital energy, sometimes the result of a stubborn chastity and also of a pro-

---

1. Baudelaire compares Poe with Denis Diderot, eighteenth-century French philosopher and art critic whose Enlightenment views stressed the rational order of nature.

foundly repressed sensibility. The unnatural pleasure that man may feel upon seeing the flow of his own blood, sudden violent, useless movements, cries uttered for no reason at all, are phenomena of the same order.

THE MOST CLASSICAL OF MODERN WRITERS

The most classical of modern writers, Poe is great because he is independent of cheap attractions, independent of sex, of patriotism, of fighting, of sentimentality, snobbery, gluttony, and all the rest of the vulgar stock-in-trade of his profession. This is what gives him his superb distinction. One vulgarized thing, the pathos of dying children, he touched in "Annabel Lee," and devulgarized it at once. He could not even amuse himself with detective stories without purifying the atmosphere of them until they became more edifying than most of Hymns, Ancient and Modern. His verse sometimes alarms and puzzles the reader by fainting with its own beauty; but the beauty is never the beauty of the flesh. You never say to him as you have to say uneasily to so many modern artists: "Yes, my friend, but these are things that men and women should *live* and not write about. Literature is not a keyhole for people with starved affections to peep through at the banquets of the body." It never became one in Poe's hands. Life cannot give you what he gives you except through fine art; and it was his instinctive observance of this distinction, and the fact that it did not beggar him, as it would beggar most writers, that makes him the most legitimate, the most classical, of modern writers.

George Bernard Shaw, *Nation*, January 16, 1909.

In the midst of the rarified art of this literature, the mind may feel the vague anguish, the fear close to tears and the uneasiness of heart which exist in vast and strange places. But admiration triumphs and the art is so great! The backgrounds and accessories are appropriate to the feelings of the characters involved. The solitude of nature or the agitation of cities, everything is described spiritedly and fantastically. Like our own Eugene Delacroix,[2] who has raised his art to the level of great poetry, Edgar Poe loves to represent agitated figures against violet or greenish backgrounds in which are revealed the phosphorescence of decay and the smell of storms. So-called inanimate nature takes on the na-

---

2. Poe's French contemporary, a pre-Impressionist painter of sometimes exotic subjects.

ture of living beings, and, like them, trembles with a supernatural and galvanic chill. . . . Sometimes magnificent vistas saturated with light and color suddenly open up in his landscapes, and at the end of the horizons are seen oriental cities and buildings, etherealized by distance, bathed in a shower of golden sunlight.

POE'S CHARACTERS

The characters in Poe, or rather the character in Poe, the man with extremely acute faculties, the man with relaxed nerves, the man whose patient and ardent will hurls defiance at difficulties, he whose gaze is fixed as straight as a sword on objects which increase in importance as he stares at them—this man is Poe himself. And his women, all luminous and sickly, dying of strange diseases and speaking with a voice which is like music, they too are Poe; or at least, through their strange aspirations, through their knowledge, through their incurable melancholy, they strongly share the nature of their creator. As for his ideal woman, she is revealed in different portraits scattered through his scant collection of poems, portraits, or rather ways of feeling beauty, which the temperament of the author joins together and blends in a vague but sensible unity, and in which exists perhaps more delicately than elsewhere that insatiable love of the Beautiful, which is his great title, that is to say the summation of his claims on the affection and admiration of poets.

Poe Is a Terrible Poet

Aldous Huxley

English author Aldous Huxley is best known for
his novel *Brave New World*, a pessimistic satire set
in a nightmarish twenty-fifth-century Utopia. He
was also a critic and writer of short stories, essays,
and nonfiction, and in his later years grew interested
in mysticism and Eastern philosophy. In the following excerpt, Huxley criticizes Poe's poetry, finding
the rhymes forced, the imagery vapid, and the alliteration obvious.

Eulalie, Ulalume, Raven and Bells, Conqueror Worm and
Haunted Palace. . . . Was Edgar Allan Poe a major poet? It
would surely never occur to any English-speaking critic to
say so. And yet, in France, from 1850 till the present time, the
best poets of each generation—yes, and the best critics, too;
for, like most excellent poets, Baudelaire, Mallarmé, Paul
Valéry are also admirable critics—have gone out of their way
to praise him. Only a year or two ago M. Valéry repeated the
now traditional French encomium of Poe, and added at the
same time a protest against the faintness of our English
praise. We who are speakers of English and not English
scholars, who were born into the language and from childhood have been pickled in its literature—we can only say,
with all due respect, that Baudelaire, Mallarmé and Valéry
are wrong and that Poe is not one of our major poets. A taint
of vulgarity spoils, for the English reader, all but two or
three of his poems—the marvellous 'City in the Sea' and 'To
Helen,' for example, whose beauty and crystal perfection
make us realize, as we read them, what a very great artist
perished on most of the occasions when Poe wrote verse. It
is to this perished artist that the French poets pay their tribute. Not being English, they are incapable of appreciating
those finer shades of vulgarity that ruin Poe for us, just as
we, not being French, are incapable of appreciating those

From Aldous Huxley, "Vulgarity in Literature," *Saturday Review of Literature*,
September 27, 1930. Reprinted by permission of D. Halsey, as agent for the Aldous L.
Huxley Literary Estate.

finer shades of lyrical beauty which are, for them, the making of La Fontaine.

The substance of Poe is refined; it is his form that is vulgar. He is, as it were, one of Nature's Gentlemen, unhappily cursed with incorrigible bad taste. To the most sensitive and high-souled man in the world we should find it hard to forgive, shall we say, the wearing of a diamond ring on every finger. Poe does the equivalent of this in his poetry; we notice the solecism and shudder. Foreign observers do not notice it; they detect only the native gentlemanliness in the poetical intention, not the vulgarity in the details of execution. To them, we seem perversely and quite incomprehensibly unjust.

TINGES OF BADNESS

It is when Poe tries to make it too poetical that his poetry takes on its peculiar tinge of badness. Protesting too much that he is a gentleman, and opulent into the bargain, he falls into vulgarity. Diamond rings on every finger proclaim the parvenu.

Consider, for example, the first two stanzas of "Ulalume."

> The skies they were ashen and sober;
>   The leaves they were crisped and sere—
>   The leaves they were withering and sere;
> It was night in the lonesome October
>   Of my most immemorial year;
> It was hard by the dim lake of Auber,
>   In the misty mid region of Weir—
> It was down by the dank tarn of Auber
>   In the ghoul-haunted woodland of Weir.
>
> Here once, through an alley Titanic,
>   Of cypress, I roamed with my soul,
>   Of cypress, with Psyche my soul.
> These were days when my heart was volcanic
>   As the scoriac rivers that roll—
>   As the lavas that restlessly roll
> Their sulphurous currents down Yaanek
>   In the ultimate clime of the pole—
> That groan as they roll down Mount Yaanek
>   In the realms of the boreal pole.

These lines protest too much (and with what a variety of voices!) that they are poetical, and, protesting, are therefore vulgar. To start with, the walloping dactylic metre is all too musical. Poetry ought to be musical, but musical with tact, subtly and variously. Metres whose rhythms, as in this case, are strong, insistent and practically invariable offer the poet a kind of short cut to musicality. They provide him (my subject calls for a mixture of metaphors) with a ready-made, reach-me-down music. He does not have to create a music appropriately modulated to his meaning; all he has to do is to shovel the meaning into the moving stream of the metre and allow the current to carry it along on waves that, like those of the best hairdressers, are guaranteed permanent. Many nineteenth-century poets used these metrical short cuts to music, with artistically fatal results.

> Then when nature around me is smiling
>   The last smile which answers to mine,
> I do not believe it beguiling,
>   Because it reminds me of thine.

How can one take even Byron seriously, when he protests his musicalness in such loud and vulgar accents? It is only by luck or an almost superhuman poetical skill that these all too musical metres can be made to sound, through their insistent barrel-organ rhythms, the intricate, personal music of the poet's own meaning. Byron occasionally, for a line or two, takes the hard kink out of those dactylic permanent waves and appears, so to speak, in his own musical hair; and Hood,[1] by an unparalleled prodigy of technique, turns even the reach-me-down music of "The Bridge of Sighs" into a personal music, made to the measure of the subject and his own emotion. Moore,[2] on the contrary, is always perfectly content with the permanent wave; and Swinburne, that super-Moore of a later generation, was also content to be a permanent waver—the most accomplished, perhaps, in all the history of literature. The complexity of his ready-made musics and his technical skill in varying the number, shape and contour of his permanent waves are simply astonishing. But, like Poe and the others, he protested too much, he tried to be too poetical. However elaborately devious his short cuts to music may be, they are still short cuts—and short cuts (this is the irony) to poetical vulgarity.

A quotation and a parody will illustrate the difference between ready-made music and music made to measure. I remember (I trust correctly) a simile of Milton's:—

>   Like that fair field
> Of Enna, where Proserpine gathering flowers,
> Herself a fairer flower, by gloomy Dis
> Was gathered, Which cost Ceres all that pain
> To seek her through the world.

1. English poet Thomas Hood wrote social-protest and comic verse.   2. Huxley criticizes Irish poet Thomas Moore's unvarying meter and singsong style.

Rearranged according to their musical phrasing, these lines would have to be written thus:—

> Like that fair field of Enna,
>   where Proserpine gathering flowers,
> Herself a fairer flower,
>   by gloomy Dis was gathered,
> Which cost Ceres all that pain
> To seek her through the world.

The contrast between the lyrical swiftness of the first four phrases, with that row of limping spondees which tells of Ceres' pain, is thrillingly appropriate. Bespoke, the music fits the sense like a glove.

IMITATING POE

How would Poe have written on the same theme? I have ventured to invent his opening stanza.

> It was noon in the fair field of Enna,
>   When Proserpina gathering flowers—
>   Herself the most fragrant of flowers,
> Was gathered away to Gehenna
>   By the Prince of Plutonian powers;
> Was born down the windings of Brenner
>   To the gloom of his amorous bowers—
> Down the tortuous highway of Brenner
>   To the God's agapemonous bowers.

The parody is not too outrageous to be critically beside the point; and anyhow the music is genuine Poe. That permanent wave is unquestionably an *ondulation de chez Edgar.* The much too musical metre is (to change the metaphor once more) like a rich chasuble, so stiff with gold and gems that it stands unsupported, a carapace of jewelled sound, into which the sense, like some snotty little seminarist, irrelevantly creeps and is lost. This music of Poe's—how much less really musical it is than that which, out of his nearly neutral decasyllables, Milton fashioned on purpose to fit the slender beauty of Proserpine, the strength and swiftness of the ravisher and her mother's heavy, despairing sorrow!

"THE RAVEN"

Of the versification of "The Raven" Poe says, in his *Philosophy of Composition:* "My first object (as usual) was originality. The extent to which this has been neglected in versification is one of the most unaccountable things in the world. Admitting that there is little possibility of variety in mere *rhythm,* it is still clear that the possible varieties of metre and stanza are absolutely infinite—and yet, *for centuries, no man, in verse, has ever done or ever seemed to think of doing an original thing."* This fact, which Poe hardly exaggerates, speaks volumes for the good sense of the poets. Feeling that almost all strikingly original metres and stanzas were only illegitimate short cuts to a music which, when reached, turned out to be but a poor and vulgar substitute for individual music, they wisely stuck to the less blatantly musical metres of tradition. The ordinary iambic decasyllable, for example, is intrinsically musical enough to be just able, when required, to stand up by itself. But its musical stiffness can easily be taken out of it. It can be now a chasuble, a golden carapace of sound, now, if the poet so desires, a pliant soft and, musically speaking, almost neutral material, out of which he can fashion a special music of his own to fit his thoughts and feelings in all their incessant transformations. Good landscape painters seldom choose a "picturesque" subject; they want to paint their own picture, not have it imposed on them by nature. In the thoroughly paintable little places of this world you will generally find only bad painters. (It's so easy to paint the thoroughly paintable.) The good ones prefer the unspectacular neutralities of the Home

---

POE'S FAME A PUZZLE

In this letter to W.T. Horton written on September 3, 1889, excerpted from Letters of W.B. Yeats, *the well-known poet expresses his dislike of Poe's work.*

[Poe's] fame always puzzles me. . . . I admire a few lyrics of his extremely and a few pages of his prose, chiefly in his critical essays, which are sometimes profound. The rest of him seems to me vulgar and commonplace and the Pit and the Pendulum and the Raven do not seem to me to have permanent literary value of any kind. Analyse the Raven and you find that its subject is a commonplace and its execution a rhythmical trick. Its rhythm never lives for a moment, never once moves with an emotional life. The whole thing seems to me insincere and vulgar. Analyse the Pit and the Pendulum and you find an appeal to the nerves by tawdry physical affrightments, at least so it seems to me who am yet puzzled at the fame of such things.

Allan Wade, ed., *Letters of W.B. Yeats.*

Counties to those Cornish coves and Ligurian fishing villages, whose picturesqueness is the delight of all those who have no pictures of their own to project on to the canvas. It is the same with poetry: good poets avoid what I may call, by analogy, 'musicesque' metres, preferring to create their own music out of raw materials as nearly as possible neutral. Only bad poets, or good poets against their better judgment, and by mistake, go to the Musicesque for their material. "For centuries no man, in verse, has ever done or ever seemed to think of doing an original thing." It remained for Poe and the other nineteenth-century metrists to do it; Procrustes-like, they tortured and amputated significance into fitting the ready-made music of their highly original metres and stanzas. The result was, in most cases, as vulgar as a Royal Academy Sunrise on Ben Nevis (with Highland Cattle) or a genuine handpainted sketch of Portofino.

How could a judge so fastidious as Baudelaire listen to Poe's music and remain unaware of its vulgarity? A happy ignorance of English versification preserved him, I fancy, from this realization. His own imitations of mediaeval hymns prove how far he was from understanding the first principles of versification in a language where the stresses are not, as in French, equal, but essentially and insistently uneven. In his Latin poems Baudelaire makes the ghost of Bernard of Cluny write as though he had learned his art from Racine. The principles of English versification are much the same as those of mediaeval Latin. If Baudelaire could discover lines composed of equally stressed syllables in Bernard, he must also have discovered them in Poe. Interpreted according to Racinian principles, such verses as

> It was down by the dank tarn of Auber
> In the ghoul-haunted woodland of Weir

must have taken on, for Baudelaire, heaven knows what exotic subtlety of rhythm. We can never hope to guess what that ghoul-haunted woodland means to a Frenchman possessing only a distant and theoretical knowledge of our language.

"ULALUME"

Returning now to "Ulalume," we find that its too poetical metre has the effect of vulgarizing by contagion what would be otherwise perfectly harmless and refined technical devices. Thus, even the very mild alliterations in "the ghoul-haunted woodland of Weir" seem to protest too much. And

yet an iambic verse beginning "Woodland of Weir, ghoul-
haunted," would not sound in the least over-poetical. It is
only in the dactylic environment that those two w's strike
one as protesting too much.

And then there are the proper names. Well used, proper
names can be relied on to produce the most thrilling musical-
magical effects. But use them without discretion, and the
magic evaporates into abracadabrical absurdity, or becomes
its own mocking parody; the over-emphatic music shrills
first into vulgarity and finally into ridiculousness. Poe tends
to place his proper names in the most conspicuous position
in the line (he uses them constantly as rhyme words), show-
ing them off—these magical-musical jewels—as the *rasta-
couaire* might display the twin cabochon emeralds at his shirt
cuffs and the platinum wrist watch, with his monogram in
diamonds. These proper-name rhyme-jewels are particularly
flashy in Poe's case because they are mostly dissyllabic. Now,
the dissyllabic rhyme in English is poetically so precious and
so conspicuous by its richness that, if it is not perfect in itself
and perfectly used, it emphatically ruins what it was meant
emphatically to adorn. Thus, sound and association make of
"Thule" a musical-magical proper name of exceptional
power. But when Poe writes,

I have reached these lands but newly
From an ultimate dim Thule,

he spoils the effect which the word ought to produce by in-
sisting too much, and incompetently, on its musicality. He
shows off his jewel as conspicuously as he can, but only reveals thereby the badness of its setting and his own Levan-
tine love of display. For "newly" does not rhyme with
"Thule"—or only rhymes on condition that you pronounce
the adverb as though you were a Bengali, or the name as
though you came from Whitechapel. The paramour of
Goethe's king rhymed perfectly with the name of his kingdom; and when Laforgue wrote of that '*roi de Thulé, Im-
maculé*' his *rime riche* was entirely above suspicion. Poe's
rich rhymes, on the contrary, are seldom above suspicion.
That dank tarn of Auber is only very dubiously a fit poetical
companion for the tenth month, and though Mount Yaanek
is, *ex hypothesi,* a volcano, the rhyme with volcanic is,
frankly, impossible. On other occasions Poe's proper names
rhyme not only well enough, but actually, in the particular
context, much too well. Dead D'Elormie, in "The Bridal Bal-

lad," is prosodically in order, because Poe had brought his ancestors over with the Conqueror (as he also imported the ancestors of that Guy de Vere who wept his tear over Lenore) for the express purpose of providing a richly musical-magical rhyme to "bore me" and "before me." Dead D'Elormie is first cousin to Edward Lear's aged Uncle Arly, sitting on a heap of Barley—ludicrous; but also (unlike dear Uncle Arly) horribly vulgar, because of the too musical lusciousness of his invented name and his display, in all tragical seriousness, of an obviously faked Norman pedigree. Dead D'Elormie is a poetical disaster.

Poe Invented the Modern Detective Story

Celestin Pierre Cambiaire

In Poe's tales of ratiocination, or detective stories, the main character always uses his intellect and not his instincts or emotions to solve the crimes he investigates. The author of the following article, Celestin Pierre Cambiaire, argues that Poe invented modern detective fiction. Though he asserts that Voltaire's *Zadig* influenced Poe, Cambiaire is nevertheless quick to credit Poe as the originator of the new genre. Cambiaire's essay, excerpted here, was written as a doctoral dissertation.

Poe did not write any detective novels, but he wrote excellent detective stories or *Tales of Ratiocination* from which according to the general consensus of opinion of the critics sprang the modern detective story not only in his own country but everywhere.

"The history of the detective story," says Brander Matthews, "begins with the publication of *The Murders in the Rue Morgue,* a masterpiece of its kind, which even its author was unable to surpass; and Poe, unlike most originators, rang the bell the first time he took aim."[1]

In the introduction to *Monsieur Dupin, The Detective Stories of E.A. Poe,* we read: "Poe is universally recognized as the father of the detective story."[2] The same critic who signs W.A.B. adds to this statement, in another page, the following: "The detective story has been originated by Poe. It transforms one phase of our social life, a phase in itself sufficiently sordid, into material for romance."[3] . . .

Writers of detective stories or novels do not hesitate in ascribing to Poe the creation of the modern detective fiction.

1. *Scribner's Magazine,* vol 42, p. 287, Sept. 1907.   2. *Monsieur Dupin, The Detective Stories of Poe*, Introduction by W.A.B. (McClure, N.Y., 1904), p. IV.   3. *Ibid.,* p. XII.

Excerpted from *The Influence of Edgar Allan Poe in France* by Celestin Pierre Cambiaire (New York: G.E. Stechert, 1927).

Doctor Doyle, as quoted by Miss Carolyn Wells in her book on *The Mystery Story*, makes the following acknowledgement:

> Edgar Allan Poe, who in his carelessly prodigal fashion threw out the seeds from which so many of our present forms of literature have sprung, was the father of the detective tale, and covered its limits so completely that I fail to see how his followers can find any fresh ground which they can confidently call their own. For the secret of the thinness and also of the intensity of the detective story is that the writer is left with only one quality, that of *intellectual acuteness,* with which to endow his hearer. Everything else is outside the picture and weakens the effect. The problem and its solution must form the theme, and the character drawing is limited and subordinate. On this narrow path the writer must walk, and he sees the footmarks of Poe always in front of him. He is happy if he ever finds the means of breaking away and striking out on some little side-track of his own.[4]

C. Alphonso Smith, one of the greatest authorities on Poe, heralds him as the founder of the modern school of detective story. This well-known critic writes:

"In the *Tales of Ratiocination,* Poe laid the foundation for the *modern school of detective stories.* In *The Murders in Rue Morgue, The Mystery of Marie Roget, The Gold Bug,* and *The Purloined Letter,* Poe solved mysteries by the detective's process of analysis."[5]

In the modern detective story the most important character is the "intellectual sleuth" who traces and discovers the criminal or the mystery. Detective fiction is indebted to Poe for the first introduction of such a character. As says Mr. Arthur Bartlett Maurice in his article on "The Detective in Fiction,"

> it was in Edgar Allan Poe's Dupin that the reasoner, the intellectual sleuth, first took definite form. Poe's weird mind had seized upon some curious phases of our mental life which are with us every day, and yet which are so vague and shadowy that they are persistently ignored.[6] He had indulged as has every one, in the tracing of one's mind back from thought to thought, and he conceived the idea of an acute observer who should reverse the process, and by a careful analysis of character and temperament, and a close watch of such outside subjects as might have influence, accurately follow from subject to subject the workings of his neighbour's mind.[7]

4. Wells Carolyn, *The Technique of the Myst. Story* (Springfield 1913), p. 63. The same citation is made in the *Anglistische Forschungen, Sherlock Holmes.* etc. by Fried. Depken, Heft 41, p. 99, Heidelberg, 1914.   5. Smith C. Alphonso *E.A. Poe,* p. 240.   6. *The Bookman* vol. 15, April 1902, "The Detective in Fiction" by A. Bartlett Maurice, p. 234.
7. *The Bookman* vol. 15, p. 234.

Thus, according to well-known authorities already quoted, Poe is the founder of the detective story, the originator of detective[8] fiction,[9] the inventor of the "intellectual[10] sleuth," and has laid "the foundation of the modern school of detective stories." Followers, imitators, disciples are indebted to those who showed them the way; hence, it seems, modern detective fiction writers in general are indebted to the great American, and the detective fiction writers of France are no exception. . . .

Speaking of Poe's contribution to the detective story Chandler says:—"His (Poe's) bibliographers have not investigated his detective fiction as to source of influences."[11]

Moreover, to use the words of the same critic, "Histories of literature ignore detective fiction, and it has been accorded but slight treatment in the magazines."[12]

However, detective fiction seems to be worth discussing. "There is as true literature in Poe's detective stories," states Miss Carolyn Wells, "as in Bacon's Essays, though of a different sort."[13]

"While human nature is what it is," asserts *The Westminster Review*, "and until the evolution of society has attained to a much higher level than it has yet reached, the subject of crime as handled, and exhibited to us by the literary artist, whether in drama or in novel, will ever have a certain fascination for the average mind."[14]

POE'S INFLUENCE ON THE FRENCH WRITERS

The famous *Tales of Ratiocination* happened to come at the opportune moment in France. "Within the realm of fiction," says Chandler, "the police hero had been long maturing; it was necessary that a Vidocq should issue his *Mémoires* (1828–1829) for the literary transition from rogue to detective to be definitely effected.[15] Balzac was indebted[16] to Vidocq for the creation of his *Vautrin* and *Vautrin* in turn inspired the plot of Dickens' *Great Expectations*.[17]

"Balzac's *Histoire des Treize* (1833–34), *Splendeurs et Misères des Courtisanes* (1838–1846), and *Ténébreuse Affaire*

---

8. See *Scribner's Magazine* vol. 42, p. 287.   9. See Smith A.C. *Poe*, p. 240.   10. See *The Bookman* vol. 15, Ap. 1902, p. 234.   11. Chandler, F. W. *The Literature of Roguery*, vol. 11, p. 549.   12. *Ibid.*   13. Wells, Carolyn, *The Technique of the Mystery Story*, p. 14. 14. *Westminster Review*, "Crime in Current Literature," vol. 147, April 1897, pp. 430, 431.   15. Chandler, Frank W., *The Literature of Roguery*, vol. 11, p. 549.   16. *Ibid.*, p. 527.   17. Chandler, F.W., *The Literature of Roguery*, pp. 527–528.

(1841) presented the police hero in various aspects. Dumas put forward M. Jackal in *Les Mohicans de Paris* as one of the earliest of the type, but Hugo's *Javert* had been conceived and drawn at nearly the same time, although *Les Misérables* did not see the light until 1862. Eugène Sue who in *Kernock le Pirate* (1830), *Les Sept Péchés capitaux* (1847–49) and similar works had begun to study rogues, wrote a criminal epic *Les Mystères de Paris* (1842–1843), which incidentally exhibits the Prince de Gerolstein assuming the role of amateur detective."

VOLTAIRE'S INFLUENCE ON POE'S WRITING

Poe, according to F. Depken,[18] drew some inspiration from Vidocq's *Mémoires*. That he had read them is evidenced by his criticism of the Frenchman:

> Vidocq, for example, was a good guesser, and a persevering man. But, without educated thought, he erred continually by the very intensity of his investigations. He impaired his vision by holding the object too close. He might see, perhaps, one or two points with unusual clearness, but in so doing he, necessarily, lost sight of the matter as a whole. Thus there is such a thing as being too profound.[19]

To use Brander Matthew's words: "The American romancer (Poe) was sufficiently familiar with the 'Human Comedy' to venture an unidentified quotation from it."[20]

However, Poe's real predecessor in detective-story writing seems to have been Voltaire. "The only predecessor with a good claim to be considered a progenitor is Voltaire," asserts Matthews, "in whose *Zadig*[21] we can find the method which Poe was to apply more elaborately." The Goncourts perceived this descent of Poe from Voltaire when they recorded in their *Journal* that the strange tales of the American poet seemed to them to belong to a "new literature, the literature of the twentieth century, scientifically miraculous storytelling by A + B, a literature at once monomaniac and mathematical, Zadig as district attorney, Cyrano de Bergerac as a pupil of Arago."[22] . . .

Whether or not Poe was in any manner indebted to Voltaire's *Zadig* it seems evident that when, through the

18. See Depken, F., *Anglistische Forschungen, Sherlock Holmes,* etc., p.71. "Ganz in Gegensatz zu Poe verliess sich Vidocq auf die Inspiration, die, wie er in seinen *Memoires* (1828–1829) selbst behauptet, ihn selten getäuscht hat. Dupin verwirft natürlich diese Methode; . . . etc."   19. Poe, *Works* (Harrison), vol. IV, p. 166, *The M. in the Rue M.*   20. *Scribner's Magazine,* Sept. 1907, B. Matthews, *Poe and the Detective Story, p.* 289.   21. *Scribner's Magazine,* vol. 42, Sept. 1907, p. 290.   22. See page 48, this study, for French quotation of Goncourts.

translation of Baudelaire, his *Tales of Ratiocination* became known to the French, they found what may be called a very well prepared ground, as they were reaching an end that several French writers have been striving to attain, and creating a new genre that had already been announced, but not perfected, and which the reading public was ready to accept with eagerness and delight.

Poe Heavily Influenced Other Writers

Jeffrey Meyers

In the following excerpt, author Jeffrey Meyers claims that Poe's greatest legacy is the influence he has had on other writers. Poe has been dubbed the father of the horror story, the mystery, and science fiction. Meyers believes the storyteller's influence can be seen in the work of some of America's best writers, including Herman Melville, F. Scott Fitzgerald, Vladimir Nabokov, and Tom Wolfe. Meyers is the author of Edgar Allan Poe: His Life and Legacy.

Poe's influence on American literature was deep and pervasive. His Gothic mystery tales had supplied European authors with new themes, images and genres, which they freely adapted to their own cultural contexts and literary forms. To Americans, Poe was an originator. With Hawthorne and Melville, he created the ambiguous opposition of good and evil that has dominated American literature. His *Narrative of Arthur Gordon Pym* was, in this context, an allegory of the American's search for dominion over himself as well as a new geographic territory, a struggle to achieve an individual and a national identity. Poe was one of the first satirists of this potentially rich society, ambitiously seeking wealth and power; and the first artist who attempted—and failed—to support himself by writing. Poe's controversial life eventually became part of the symbolic meaning of his work.

POE'S INFLUENCE ON MELVILLE

Though Melville never mentioned *Pym* and there is no concrete evidence that he had read it, there are, as Patrick Quinn has pointed out, striking similarities that suggest the influence of Poe's book on *Moby-Dick* (1851). Both writers used the works of Jeremiah Reynolds as a common source.

Poe's opening sentence: "My name is Arthur Gordon Pym" becomes more dramatic, immediate and familiar in Melville's "Call me Ishmael." Pym and Ishmael each have a ferocious, exotic, half-savage comrade who saves his life. Both are narrators of as well as participants in a dangerous sea voyage. Pym's journey culminates in a confrontation with an enigmatic evil, a menacing white being in a strange white sea. While the purpose of Pym's journey is not defined, Melville's Ahab seeks a definite goal—the destruction of Moby-Dick, the white whale that represents both untamed nature and the evil in Ahab himself. Pym risks his life, nearly dying of dehydration, suffocation, ambush or capture; but he pursues his journey, like the crew of the *Pequod*, toward the white blankness of the end. Melville's comment on the sinister atmosphere of *Moby-Dick* applies with equal force to Poe's *Pym:* "A polar wind blows through it, & birds of prey hover over it." Just as Poe's stories of revenge, murder and remorse influenced the more elaborate novels of Dostoyevsky, so his incomplete tale of an imaginary voyage doubtless helped Melville create his American masterpiece.

POE AND FITZGERALD

In the twentieth century American novelists have used Poe's satiric as well as symbolic elements. Scott Fitzgerald, casting his moral fable of youthful obsession with the rich and disillusion with money in the form of a fantasy, deliberately imitated and parodied Poe's most famous story, "The Fall of the House of Usher" in "The Diamond as Big as the Ritz" (1922). Fitzgerald was not only influenced by Poe's literary works, but was also acutely aware of the parallels between Poe's life and his own.

Both had eminent ancestors (Poe's grandfather was a Quartermaster in the Revolutionary Army, Fitzgerald was descended from the patriotic poet Francis Scott Key), but since Poe's parents were impoverished actors and Fitzgerald's father a pathetic failure, each writer, uneasy about his social status, was powerfully attracted to old families and envied solid wealth. Though Poe was born in Boston and Fitzgerald in St. Paul, they associated themselves with the Southern gentility and courtly manners of Virginia (where Poe grew up) and of Maryland (where Fitzgerald's father was raised). Poe left the University of Virginia, as Fitzgerald left Princeton, without graduating. After serving as an enlisted man, Poe was expelled from West Point; Fitzgerald had an equally undistinguished career in American military camps and never crossed the ocean to fight in the European war. He strongly identified with and even imitated Poe's life, and spoke for both of them when he said: "I talk with the authority of failure."

Both men had tragic marriages. Virginia Poe died of tuberculosis at the age of twenty-four; Zelda Fitzgerald became insane when she was twenty-nine. Both men wasted their artistic talents as hack writers for popular magazines, yet were desperately short of money and frequently had to borrow from their friends. Alcoholics who became intoxicated after one or two glasses, they often lost control of themselves, behaved in an abject and humiliating manner, and remained drunk for a week at a time. Poe ruined his career by offending literary editors just as Fitzgerald did with powerful film producers. Both authors died from the effects of drink and were buried in the state of Maryland. Their reckless personal behavior seriously damaged their literary reputations, which were not revived until many years after their deaths.

It is not surprising, then, given Fitzgerald's lifelong identification with Poe, that he should have sought in Poe's well-known story a Gothic setting and a fantastic form that would express his own ambivalent feelings about the rich. Though Poe characteristically emphasizes the decay and horror, Fitzgerald the glamour and luxury of the house; Poe's heroine is diseased and moribund, Fitzgerald's "the incarnation of physical perfection"; Poe has a tragic, Fitzgerald an apparently happy ending, the numerous parallels, once perceived, are unmistakable.

Fitzgerald echoes the name of Poe's Usher by calling his hero Unger. In both stories a young man, Poe's narrator and Fitzgerald's naive schoolboy, is invited to visit an "intimate" boyhood friend. The neurasthenic Roderick Usher comes from an ancient family, and Percy Washington boasts to the provincial Unger that his father is the richest man in the world. Both visitors represent a conventional ordinariness, a certain norm of behavior that helps to define the bizarre nature of the events they observe.

The narrator in Poe and the naive hero in Fitzgerald see their friends as part of a doomed family in a cursed house. Both mansions have intricate subterranean passages and are remote, isolated and fantastically unreal. Situated near a tarn or lake, each monstrous house contains an oppressive secret, and reflects the fearful mood of its inhabitants.

Poe's hothouse rhetoric: "What was it—I paused to think—what was it that so unnerved me in the contemplation of the House of Usher?" is echoed in John Unger's troubled questions when he first arrives at the mountain house: "What desperate transaction lay hidden here? What moral expedient of a bizarre Croesus? What terrible and golden mystery?" Poe mentions the sentience of vegetable matter—the proliferating fungi that overspread and the decayed trees that surround the house—which reflects the doom of the family. Fitzgerald imitates the idea of the house as prison by describing an old family trapped, stupefied and corrupted by its selfish accumulation of useless wealth and by the enormous diamond that cannot be sold lest it destroy the economic foundations of the world.

Roderick Usher's dissipated artistic endeavors—his dreary dirges, phantasmagoric paintings and morbid poetry—are reflected in Fitzgerald by a kidnapped "landscape gardener, an architect, a designer of stage settings, and a French decadent poet" who fail to create as expected, go mad and are confined to a mental asylum. Only a crude "moving picture fella" from Hollywood succeeds in designing the lavish reception rooms and luxurious baths.

Both visitors briefly glimpse their host's sister as she passes through the house. Madeline Usher is cursed by a secret sexual guilt she shares with her brother. Kismine Washington (Unger's girlfriend and *kismet*, or fate) is cursed by the murder of the friends who had visited her in the past, could not be permitted to betray the secret wealth to the outside world and were sacrificed after they had provided distraction and pleasure for the family.

Fitzgerald echoes the premature entombment of Madeline in one of the numerous vaults beneath the House of Usher in Braddock Washington's incarceration of the captured aviators in a deep, Poe-like pit, covered by an iron grating. Both young men are suddenly awakened in the middle of the night by a strange, frightening noise. Poe's familiar physiological description of fear when Usher realizes he has entombed the living Madeline:

> there came a strong shudder over his whole person; a sickly smile quivered about his lips; and I saw that he spoke in a

low, hurried, and gibbering manner,

is equaled by Fitzgerald's fantastic simile when Unger perceives that the Washingtons have murdered their guests:

> Stunned with the horror of this revelation, John sat there open-mouthed, feeling the nerves of his body twitter like so many sparrows perched upon his spinal column.

In Poe, Usher throws back the ebony jaws of the huge antique panels to reveal his vengeful, bloodstained sister. In Fitzgerald, the ebony panel of one wall slides aside to reveal a uniformed manservant who assists Unger with his bath. Madeline murders her brother; Percy Washington's grandfather was also compelled to murder his brother, who had the unfortunate Poe-and-Fitzgerald-like habit "of drinking himself into an indiscreet stupor." At the end of both stories the evil houses are completely destroyed, but the visitors escape disaster.

Both stories are moral fables that offer a purely external portrayal of the characters and express the quintessential theme of illusion and reality. In "The Fall of the House of Usher," the decaying mansion symbolizes the perhaps unconscious incestuous and necrophilic desires of the Usher twins, Roderick and Madeline, who are finally rent asunder (like the house itself), after "he had to kill something inside himself" and she had to commit retributive murder. If the Ushers' sin is incest, the Washingtons' is greed; and both sins lead to the final destruction of their family, dynasty and class. Poe's narrator, who never reveals why Roderick entombed Madeline or why she murdered him, merely records the events and expresses his abstract horror. Fitzgerald, building on Poe's story, shows his hero moving from sheer enjoyment of the overwhelming luxury to an awareness of evil in the House of Washington, to a condemnation of its perverse corruption. Fitzgerald indicates, by the name of the family, that his purpose is allegorical and satiric. The House of Washington represents a vulgar, venal, greedy America where everything—freedom, human values, art and culture—is sacrificed to gross wealth. Just as Melville developed many of the themes of *Pym*, so Fitzgerald expressed the latent symbolism of "The Fall of the House of Usher."

POE AND NABOKOV

The personality and ideas of Poe made a deep impression on Vladimir Nabokov soon after he came to America. His story,

"A Forgotten Poet" (1944), was directly inspired by Poe. In this wry tale, "a Russian poet, supposed drowned at twenty-four in 1849, turns up as a seventy-four-year-old at a memorial gathering in 1899 on the fiftieth anniversary of his death, and demands the money that had been raised for a monument in his name." The noun in the title and the name of the main character, the talented poet Perov, both include the letters of Poe's name. The dates are important to Nabokov, who was as keen as Poe on puzzles, coincidences and codes. Poe also died impoverished in 1849; and the fiftieth anniversary of his death was the year of Nabokov's birth. Like Perov, Poe's reputation plunged immediately after his death, and *his* tomb was dedicated at a memorial gathering in 1875.

Like Poe, Nabokov knew what it was like to struggle with poverty during the years following his exile from Russia, when he lived from hand to mouth in Berlin and Paris. He no doubt sympathized with Poe's shabby dignity as he went the rounds of editors and offices trying to get work. Like Perov, Poe would have preferred some cash in his lifetime to a marble monument after his death.

Nabokov admired Poe's doctrine of pure art, detached from moral freight. He translated Poe's story "Silence—A Fable" into Russian, and echoed the phrase "the ghoul-haunted woodland of Weir" from "Ulalume" in *Bend Sinister*'s "the ghoul-haunted Province of Perm." Considering his professional interest in entomology, it is a pity that Nabokov did not carefully investigate the taxonomy of Poe's Gold-Bug as he had of Kafka's monstrous dung beetle.

Nabokov's best novel, *Lolita* (1955), shows Poe's influence most strongly. He originally called it *The Kingdom by the Sea,* an allusion to "Annabel Lee," and made dozens of references to Poe throughout the novel. Humbert's obsession with the pubescent nymphet Lolita—revealed first in a small town and then, as they travel by car, in the vast transcontinental landscape—is an ironic recreation of Poe's strange marriage to his adolescent cousin. "Did she have a precursor?" Humbert remarks. "She did, indeed, she did. In point of fact there might have been no Lolita at all had I not loved, one summer, a certain initial girl-child. In a princedom by the sea." The strange metamorphosis of the slim, Southern Edgar into another awkward outsider, the middle-aged European Humbert, and of the childish, dying Virginia into the naive yet knowing Lolita, is as brilliantly original as anything in Poe. Nabokov's novel uses Poe's life and works to satirize the meaningless conventions and philistine values of bourgeois American society.

POE AND TOM WOLFE

Just as Fitzgerald had used Poe's story to portray the corruption in American life, so Tom Wolfe, in his novel *The Bonfire of the Vanities* (1987), called one chapter "The Masque of the Red Death" to suggest the rottenness of the New York rich. Instead of a masked ball, the scene is a dinner party at the Bavardages, where Lord Buffing, an elderly English poet, rises to address the guests. Invoking the memory of Poe and his poetry, he states that our art is finished and that we can no longer write: "we poets no longer even have the vitality to write epics. We don't even have the courage to make rhymes, and the American epic should have rhymes, rhyme on top of rhyme in a shameless cascade, rhymes of the sort that Edgar Allan Poe gave us." In Buffing's view, Poe is the archetype of the fevered visionary, the prophet despised in his own land:

> Poe, who lived his last years just north of here, I believe, in a part of New York called the Bronx . . . in a little cottage with lilacs and a cherry tree . . . and a wife dying of tuberculosis. A drunk he was, of course, perhaps a psychotic—but with the madness of prophetic vision. He wrote a story that tells all we need to know about the moment we live in now.

Lord Buffing, who knows he is dying of AIDS, represents the masqued figure in Poe's story who enters disguised as death and whose touch is fatal. Like Prince Prospero and his revelers, these New Yorkers are cut off from the poverty that surrounds them. But AIDS, the spectral curse and modern plague, is among them. Lord Buffing narrates Poe's story, emphasizing how the guests are irresistibly drawn toward the room where Death awaits them, for

> families, homes, children, the great chain of being, the eternal tide of chromosomes mean nothing to them any longer. . . . So Poe was kind enough to write the ending for us more than a hundred years ago. Knowing that, who can possibly write all the sunnier passages that should come before? Not I, not I. The sickness—the nausea—the pitiless pain—have ceased with the fever that maddened my brain—with the fever called "Living"—those were among the last words he wrote.

Wolfe uses Poe's story and his lyric "For Annie" to create an atmosphere of hysteria and fear, a sense of impending doom. This contrasts in the novel with the blind narcissism of the characters, who react to the old man's speech with embarrassed silence. Poe's pathological imagery of sickness, nausea and maddening fever, based on his observation of the ravages of tuberculosis, poignantly suggests the symptoms of AIDS.

Wolfe used "The Masque of the Red Death" to stress the meaningless pursuit of wealth, the self-destruction of the most talented artists and the doom-laden quality of American society. Just as Poe remains the quintessential example of the struggling American writer, so his suggestive stories remain an inexhaustible repository of meaning for his American followers.

Neither Poe's mannered Latinate style nor his highly idiosyncratic content became a *direct* model for subsequent poetry or prose (as Pound said: "no one who has tried to write like Poe . . . has done anything good"). Yet his extensive influence on later writers has been quite out of proportion to the extremely uneven quality of his hundred poems and seventy stories. Though Poe has always appealed to popular taste, his originality and imagination have also had a considerable impact on the most advanced thinkers and most serious writers. Poe has overcome his notorious reputation (which today makes him interesting rather than repulsive), survived the vicissitudes of art during the last hundred and fifty years and remained contemporary because he has always appealed to basic human feelings and expressed universal themes common to all men in all languages: dreams, love, loss; grief, mourning, alienation; terror, revenge, murder; insanity, disease and death.

Poe's Theatricality Is Essential to His Work

W.H. Auden

Although British-born, W. H. Auden is considered an American poet. In the following article, Auden notes that not one of Poe's narrators could possibly be considered a realistic, normal person who could function in the world. Auden argues that his characters' theatricality and exaggerated emotions are essential to his work—Poe wants to create drama on the operatic, not the realistic, scale.

What every author hopes to receive from posterity—a hope usually disappointed—is justice. Next to oblivion, the two fates which he most fears are becoming the name attached to two or three famous pieces while the rest of his work is unread and becoming the idol of a small circle which reads every word he wrote with the same uncritical reverence. The first fate is unjust because, even if the pieces known are indeed his best work, the reader has not earned the right to say so; the second fate is embarrassing and ridiculous, for no author believes he is that good.

Poe's shade must be more disappointed than most. Certain pieces—how he must hate these old war horses—are probably more familiar to non-Americans than are any pieces by any other American author. I myself cannot remember hearing any poetry before hearing "The Raven" and "The Bells"; and *The Pit and the Pendulum* was one of the first short stories I ever read. At the same time, the known works of no other author of comparable rank and productivity are so few and so invariably the same. For example, I asked a number of persons whom I knew to be widely read, but not specialists in American letters, if they had read *Gordon Pym* and *Eureka*, which seem to me to rank among Poe's most important works; not one of them had. On the other hand, I was informed by everyone that to omit *The Cask of Amontillado* [from a selection of works], which for my taste is an inferior story,. would be commercial suicide. Poor Poe! At first so forgotten that his grave went without a tombstone twenty-six years—when one was finally erected the only American author to attend the ceremony was Whitman; and today in danger of becoming the life study of a few professors. The professors are, of course, very necessary, for it is through their devoted labors that Poe may finally reach the kind of reader every author hopes for, who will read him all, good-humoredly willing to wade through much which is dull or inferior for the delight of discovering something new and admirable.

THE TALES

Varied in subject, treatment, style as Poe's stories are, they have one negative characteristic in common. There is no place in any of them for the human individual as he actually exists in space and time, that is, as simultaneously a natural creature subject in his feelings to the influences and limitations of the natural order, and an historical person, creating novelty and relations by his free choice and modified in unforeseen ways by the choices of others.

Poe's major stories fall roughly into two groups. The first group is concerned with states of willful being, the destructive passion of the lonely ego to merge with the ego of another (*Ligeia*), the passion of the conscious ego to be objective, to discover by pure reason the true relationships which sensory appearances and emotions would conceal (*The Purloined Letter*), self-destructive states in which the ego and the self are passionately hostile (*The Imp of the Perverse*), even the state of chimerical passion, that is, the passionate unrest of a self that lacks all passion (*The Man of the Crowd*). The horror tales and the tales of ratiocination belong together, for the heroes of both exist as unitary states— Roderick Usher reasons as little as Auguste Dupin feels. Personages who are the embodiment of such states cannot, of course, change or vary in intensity either through changes in themselves or their environment. The problem in writing stories of this kind is to prevent the reader from ever being reminded of historical existence, for, if he once thinks of real people whose passions are interrupted by a need for lunch or whose beauty can be temporarily and mildly impaired by the common cold, the intensity and timelessness become immediately comic. Poe is sometimes attacked for the operatic quality of the prose and *décor* in his tales, but they are essential to preserving the illusion. His heroes cannot exist except operatically. Take, for example, the following sentence from *William Wilson*:

> Let it suffice, that among spendthrifts I out-heroded Herod, and that, giving name to a multitude of novel follies, I added no brief appendix to the long catalogue of vices then usual in the most dissolute university of Europe.

In isolation, as a prose sentence, it is terrible, vague, verbose, the sense at the mercy of a conventional rhetorical rhythm. But dramatically, how right; how well it reveals the William Wilson who narrates the story in his real colors, as the fantastic self who hates and refuses contact with reality. Some of Poe's successors in stories about states of being, D.H. Lawrence for example, have tried to be nonrealistic with fatal results.

ADVENTURE STORIES

In the second group, which includes such tales as *A Descent into the Maelström* and *Gordon Pym*, the relation of will to environment is reversed. While in the first group everything that happens is the consequence of a volition upon the freedom of which there are no natural limits, in these stories of pure adventure the hero is as purely passive as the I in dreams; nothing that happens is the result of his personal choice, everything happens *to* him. What the subject feels— interest, excitement, terror—are caused by events over which he has no control whatsoever. The first kind of hero has no history because he refuses to change with time; this kind has none because he cannot change, he can only experience.

The problem for the writer of adventure stories is to invent a succession of events which are both interesting and varied and to make the order of succession plausible. To secure variety without sacrificing coherence or vice versa is more difficult than it looks, and *Gordon Pym*, one of the finest adventure stories ever written, is an object lesson in the art. Every kind of adventure occurs—adventures of natural origin like shipwreck; adventures like mutiny, caused by familiar human beings, or, like the adventures on the island, by strange natives; and, finally, supernatural nightmare events—yet each leads credibly into the next. While in the stories of passionate states a certain vagueness of description is essential to the illusion, in the adventure story credibility is secured by the minutest details, figures, diagrams, and various other devices, as in Poe's description of the mysterious ravines.

> The total length of this chasm, commencing at the opening *a* and proceeding round the corner *b* to the extremity *d*, is five hundred and fifty yards.

Both these types of Poe story have had an extraordinary influence. His portraits of abnormal or self-destructive states contributed much to Dostoyevski, his ratiocinating hero is the ancestor of Sherlock Holmes and his many successors, his tales of the future lead to H.G. Wells, his adventure stories to Jules Verne and Stevenson. It is not without interest that the development of such fiction in which the historical individual is missing should have coincided with the development of history as a science, with its own laws, and the appearance of the great nineteenth-century historians; further, that both these developments should accompany the industrialization and urbanization of social life in which the individual seems more and more the creation of historical forces while he himself feels less and less capable of affecting his life by any historical choice of his own. . . .

THE POEMS

Poe's best poems are not his most typical or original. . . . His difficulty as a poet was that he was interested in too many poetic problems and experiments at once for the time he had to give to them. To make the result conform to the intention —and the more experimental the intention, the more this is true—a writer has to keep his hand in by continual practice. The prose writer who must earn his living has this advantage, that even the purest hack work is practice in his craft; for the penniless poet there is no corresponding exercise. Without the leisure to write and rewrite he cannot develop to his full stature. When we find fault with Poe's poems we must never forget his own sad preface to them.

> In defence of my own taste, it is incumbent upon me to say that I think nothing in this volume of much value to the public, or very creditable to myself. Events not to be controlled have prevented me from making, at any time, any serious effort in what, under happier circumstances, would have been the field of my choice.

For faulty they must be admitted to be. The trouble with "The Raven," for example, is that the thematic interest and the prosodic interest, both of which are considerable, do not combine and are even often at odds.

In *The Philosophy of Composition* Poe discusses his difficulties in preventing the poem from becoming absurd and artificial. The artificiality of the lover asking the proper series of questions to which the refrain would be appropriate could be solved by making him a self-torturer. The difficulty of the speaker of the refrain, however, remained insoluble until the poet hit on the notion of something nonhuman. But the effect could still be ruined unless the narration of the story, as distinct from the questions and answers, flowed naturally; and the meter Poe chose, with its frequent feminine rhymes, so rare in English, works against this and at times defeats him.

> Not the least obeisance made he; not a minute stopped or
> stayed he;
> But with mien of lord or lady, perched above my chamber
> door.

Here it is the meter alone and nothing in the speaker or the situation which is responsible for the redundant alternatives of "stopped or stayed he" and "lord or lady."

Similarly, "Ulalume" is an interesting experiment in diction but only an experiment, for the poem is about something which never quite gets said because the sense is sacrificed to the vowel sounds. Edward Lear, the only poet, apparently, to be directly influenced by Poe, succeeds with his emotive place names, "The Hills of the Chankly Bore," where Poe fails because he selects a subject where the accidental quality of the name is part of the intended effect. "The Bells," though much less interesting a conception than "Ulalume," is more successful because the subject is nothing but an excuse for onomatopoeic effects.

EUREKA

There remains, however, *Eureka*. The man who had flatly asserted that no poem should much exceed a hundred lines in length—"that music (in its modifications of rhythm and rhyme) is of so vast a moment to Poesy as never to be neglected by him who is truly poetical," that neither Truth, the satisfaction of the Intellect, nor Passion, the excitement of the Heart, are the province of Poetry but only Beauty, and that the most poetical topic in the world is the death of a beautiful woman—this man produces at the end of his life a work which he insists is a poem and commends to posterity as his crowning achievement, though it violates every article in his critical creed. It is many pages in length, it is written in prose, it handles scientific ideas in the truth of which the poet is passionately convinced, and the general subject is the origin and destiny of the universe.

Outside France the poem has been neglected, but I do not think Poe was wrong in the importance he attached to it. In the first place, it was a very daring and original notion to take the oldest of the poetic themes—older even than the story of the epic hero—namely, cosmology, the story of how things came to exist as they do, and treat it in a completely contemporary way, to do in English in the nineteenth century what Hesiod and Lucretius had done in Greek and Latin centuries before. Secondly, it is full of remarkable intuitive guesses that subsequent scientific discoveries have confirmed. As Paul Valéry says:

> It would not be exaggerating its importance to recognize, in his theory of consistency, a fairly definite attempt to describe the universe by its *intrinsic properties.* The following proposition can be found toward the end of *Eureka:* "Each law of nature depends at all points on all the other laws." This might easily be considered, if not as a formula, at least as the expression of a tendency toward generalized relativity.

> That its tendency approaches recent conceptions becomes evident when one discovers, in the poem under discussion, an affirmation of the *symmetrical* and reciprocal relationship of matter, time, space, gravity, and light.

Lastly, it combines in one work nearly all of Poe's characteristic obsessions: the passion for merging in union with the one which is at the root of tales like *Ligeia,* the passion for logic which dominates the detective and cryptographic studies, the passion for a final explanation and reconciliation which informs the melancholy of much of his verse— all are brought together in this poem of which the prose is as lucid, as untheatrical, as the best of his critical prose. . . .

POE'S PERSONALITY

If the Muses could lobby for their interest, all biographical research into the lives of artists would probably be prohibited by law, and historians of the individual would have to confine themselves to those who act but do not make—

generals, criminals, eccentrics, courtesans, and the like, about whom information is not only more interesting but less misleading. Good artists—the artist *manqué is* another matter—never make satisfactory heroes for novelists, because their life stories, even when interesting in themselves, are peripheral and less significant than their productions. . . .

As to his private life and personality, had it been more romantically wicked, his work would not have the importance it has as being, in some senses, the first modern work. He was one of the first to suffer *consciously* the impact of the destruction of the traditional community and its values, and he paid the heaviest price for this consciousness. As D.H. Lawrence says in an essay conspicuous for its insights:

> Poe had a pretty bitter doom. Doomed to seethe down his soul in a great continuous convulsion of disintegration, and doomed to register the process. And then doomed to be abused for it, when he had performed some of the bitterest tasks of human experience, that can be asked of a man. Necessary tasks too. For the human soul must suffer its own disintegration, consciously, if ever it is to survive.

To which one might add: "Abused?" No, a worse doom than that. Doomed to be used in school textbooks as a bait to interest the young in good literature, to be a respectable rival to the pulps.

Still, he has had some rewards. Not many authors have been invoked as intercessors with God in an hour of need, as Poe was named by Baudelaire when he felt himself going mad; not many have been celebrated in poems as beautiful as Mallarmé's Sonnet.

Poe's Genius Was in Creating a Self and a Style

N. Bryllion Fagin

N. Bryllion Fagin was an associate professor of English and Drama at Johns Hopkins University in Baltimore, Maryland, when he wrote *The Histrionic Mr. Poe*, from which the following selection is taken. Fagin argues that Poe consciously created a histrionic, theatrical personality for himself that his main fictional characters duplicate. Poe fashioned his tales and personality after the prevailing romanticism of the time. It is this conscious creation that remains Poe's great appeal to this day.

Edgar Allan Poe was a singer of songs and a teller of tales, and it is understandable that he should have inspired many rhapsodies in verse and prose. It is less understandable that he should have also inspired so many biographical and critical studies which are either unbearably heavy or merely thin air.... It evidently was decided a long time ago that Poe's life was one of unrelieved tragedy and that anyone undertaking to write about him was therefore bound by the amenities to employ a tone of mournful seriousness.

Poe himself was, of course, largely responsible for this. He insisted on the tragic tone: in garb, word, voice, and exclamation point. But Poe, I have a notion, enjoyed his tone. Gravity and tragedy became him even more than mourning became Electra. One can almost see him laboring to achieve that tone, and glorying in the result of his labors. Poe was always, by his own testimony, a conscious artist.

Some years ago Edward Shanks justified his writing of a book on Poe on the ground that Poe was "the man through whom was made America's first great contribution to the literature of the world." My own justification may be that Poe

Excerpted from *The Histrionic Mr. Poe* by N. Bryllion Fagin, pp. vii-x, 24-32, 58-66. Copyright ©1949 by The Johns Hopkins University Press. Reprinted by permission of the publisher.

has himself become literature—myth, romance, poetry. To try to understand the nature of this myth, the personality of this romance, the texture of this poetry, seems to me an aim which needs no other justification. . . .

A Histrionic Impulse

The theatrical quality of much of [Poe's] behavior in life has been casually noted by many writers on Poe, but it has not received the detailed attention it deserves. The numerous facets of its expression have never been brought together and placed under focus. I believe that greater recognition of this quality may to some extent dispel the almost intolerable gloom with which Poe has come to be associated in our minds. After all, the histrio may, like any mortal, suffer the slings and arrows of fate, but he has the gift of turning his suffering into a weapon of self-defense. By means of word and gesture and pose he achieves self-importance and exaltation. Seen thus, not a little of Poe's unhappiness appears to have been mere inflation, the swellings of high performance, in which art enlarged upon reality.

And if Poe's behavior in actual everyday life—cabbin'd, cribb'd, and confined—was not devoid of the compensations any artist derives from performing well, shall we overlook the even greater compensations derived from performing in the unconfined world of the imagination? For Poe's literary work was to a remarkable extent an expression of the same histrionic impulse. Many of his poems, stories, and essays are quite clearly theatrical performances. To admit this is not to reflect on their value as works of the imagination: art has many faces and many moods. It is no small tribute to Edgar Allan Poe to say that he was the master of a certain type of literature: and precisely because his own face and mood haunt his creations. No matter that the face is sometimes a tragic mask and the mood the ingenious result of stage magic. In the end, what he has bequeathed to us is none the less art, and art of a high order. . . .

Edgar Allan Poe was a highly gifted writer. His stories are imaginative and his poems are musical. In both *genres* he was impressively romantic. The effect of his work upon the imagination is vivid and haunting. Yet to attribute the extraordinary impression he has left behind him solely to the qualities of his work would be erroneous. Shelley was imaginative and romantic; Keats was vivid and musical; but their fascination is purely that of the excellence of their work, and is confined to lovers of poetry. Only Byron somewhat approximates Poe's appeal, and it is significant that Poe as a youngster was strongly stimulated by the dramatic character of Byron's personality and writings. He felt impelled not only to emulation in verse, but also to a successful imitation of Byron's swimming exploit: six or seven miles against the tide in the James River—duplicating the British poet's feat of swimming across the Hellespont.

It is Poe's personality which has remained the inexplicable yet tangible core of his appeal. He was and still is a tantalizing mystery. Our emotional or critical attitude toward his work seems to have only a slight and remote connection with our warm curiosity. Even if we perceive some justice in Henry James's carefully shaded self-congratulation—"An enthusiasm for Poe is the mark of a decidedly primitive stage of reflection"—we nevertheless do not abandon Poe. No more than Yvor Winters did when he publicly confessed several years ago, for himself and his friends, that Poe had long passed casually, with him and with them, "as a bad writer accidentally and temporarily popular." A psychologist might accept the act of confession itself as a disclosure of preoccupation. . . .

Whether there was—and still is—an element of the "accidental" in Poe's popularity is largely a matter of semantics. If the sum total of physical and psychological equipments, aptitudes, and patterns of behavior which constitute personality be merely accidental to a writer's work, then Poe's appeal has been "accidental." But we are still baffled by the man, and the attempts of some of the best minds to explain him have intensified rather than lessened our interest. . . . Poe will continue to haunt us and to raise questions. Perhaps all we shall ever know definitely is the indubitable fact noted by a reviewer of Harrison's *Life*, away back in 1903, that "Edgar Allan Poe is the most interesting and picturesque figure in American letters."

That reviewer, Jeannette L. Gilder, justified her use of the adjective "picturesque" by adding, "because of his weaknesses and misfortunes."[1] She was partly right. Poe's weaknesses and misfortunes have contributed to his picturesqueness. The element of pathos, if not tragedy, always hovered above him, like a dark halo: Orphaned as a child; sent to the

1. "Poe Not as Black as He Was Painted," *Critic*, XLII, p. 499.

university, but, alas, for one brief year; dismissed from West Point; deserted by the girl he loved; yoked to a child-wife, frail, consumptive, who died leaving him ill and lonely; and always poverty trailing him like a lean beast throughout his life; and, the crowning stroke of fate, his death—alone, unknown—in a charitable institution. Add to that his "weaknesses"—a predisposition to alcohol, a sensitive nervous organism, instability, irritability, inordinate pride perpetually wounded, physical pain necessitating the anodyne of alcohol or opium.

ROMANCING MISERY

But add also Poe's unerring sense of romantic effectiveness. Consciously or by intuition he turned his weaknesses and misfortunes into assets. His letters teem with laments and complaints, with bitter outcries against an unjust fate, with proud defiance of a callous world, and with almost rhapsodic indulgence in self-pity. . . .

If Poe managed, in one mood or another, to call attention to his misfortunes, he managed equally well, in one key or another, to dramatize his weaknesses. In 1835 he writes to his friend and benefactor, J.P. Kennedy, that he is suffering from a spell of melancholy which he is unable to account for, as his financial condition, at the moment, is rather good and the prospects of future prosperity are even better. He is wretched and knows not why. "Convince me," he pleads, "that it is worth one's while—that it is at all necessary to live." One tell-tale sentence slips into this letter: "I say you will believe me, and for this simple reason, that a man who is writing for effect does not write *thus.*" This hardly requires the analytical powers of a M. Dupin to draw the obvious inference that Poe was aware of the possibility that his writing might produce an effect he did not intend to produce.

It is not, however, until thirteen years later, during his unsmooth courtship of Mrs. Whitman that he attempts to do something about this feeling that it is not at all necessary to live. He buys two ounces of laudanum, writes to "Annie" imploring her to come to his death bed, and then swallows "about half " the laudanum. The amount is not enough to end his life, but it is enough to make him deathly sick. In the hysterical letter in which, several days later, he tells her the story, he renews his request that she come to him. "I am so *ill,*" he concludes; "so terribly, hopelessly ILL in body and mind, that I feel I CANNOT live, unless I can feel your sweet, gentle, loving hand pressed upon my forehead."[2]

To Mrs. Whitman, who insisted on his curbing one of his weaknesses before she would consent to marry him, he confessed: "I have absolutely no pleasure in the stimulants in which I sometimes so madly indulge. It has not been in the pursuit of pleasure that I have periled life and reputation and reason. It has been a desperate attempt to escape from torturing memories." Perhaps the medical comment of Dr. John W. Robertson, one of Poe's friendliest biographers, is the only one that can be made on this confession: "If there were 'memories,' they were of prenatal inheritance."[3]...

Poe obviously believed his passionate assertions each time he made them, and he died believing them. On his last visit to Richmond he told his friend Dr. Carter that if people would not tempt him, he would not fall. He declared, " in the most solemn manner," that he *would* restrain himself.[4] Indeed, he was so confident that he *could* restrain himself that he took a pledge of total abstinence and became a member of the Order of Sons of Temperance, thereby gladdening the hearts of the "best" people of Richmond, as one clerical gentleman later recalled.[5] Several days later he lay fatally ill in Baltimore. . . . What seems strange is that he made his biographers believe his explanations and avowals. That certainly is a tribute to the persuasiveness of his style, to his ability to make any moment vivid and complete.

LITERATURE AND LIFE

Attempts to explain any creative gift are generally unconvincing, if not fatuous. In the case, however, of Poe's ability to present any moment as a complete experience, acquaintance with the whole history of the man can be very helpful. The concentration he managed to bestow upon any situation or mood is strikingly akin to that which one observes—or forgets to observe—in tense moments on a theatre stage. A gifted actor interpreting a part enters into his rôle with such intensity—even when controlled by artistic discipline—that each moment is a unique experience. There is no question of contradiction or affirmation of what has preceded; there

2. Arthur Hobson Quinn, *Edgar Allan Poe: A Critical Biography.* New York, 1941, pp. 589–592.   3. *Edgar Allan Poe: A Psychopathic Study.* New York, 1923, p. 92.   4. Susan Archer Weiss, "Last Days of Edgar A. Poe," *Scribner's Monthly,* XV, March 1878, pp. 707–716.   5. Bishop O.P. Fitzgerald, "The Night I Saw and Heard Edgar Allan Poe," in *Fifty Years,* p. 192.

is only an enactment of each scene, confrontation, or dramatic unit with such self-absorbed concentration as to render it roundly complete. . . .

ROMANTICISM AND POE'S WORK

In the light of these characteristics and abilities of the man, the circumstances of his life, and the nature of the reaction of the "world" upon which he played, the "mystery" of Poe becomes considerably less mystifying. In one way, the time and the man met. The age of Romanticism supplied an appropriate setting for his histrionic personality and his particular form of art. The description of the German romantic actor of the period which appears in Karl Mantzius's *History of Theatrical Art* is, in most respects, as vivid a sketch of Edgar Allan Poe as if the Danish historian had had the American literary histrio "sitting" for him: "A strange being, with long, wild hair, black if possible, framing a pale, emaciated face; deep, melancholy eyes under dark, contracted brows, and a bitter, sorrowful smile on his quivering lips; his form . . . moving among his fellow men now with ostentatious, gloomy remoteness, now with hollow, rather scornful mirth."[6] This is Roderick Usher, and the numerous "I's" of Poe's other stories; it is, except for the wild hair, Poe himself.

But in another way, the time for Romanticism is never completely at an end. The appeal of a Poe has always been that of an unfortunate, lonely, remote, misprized genius. "In those days," Mantzius goes on to say, speaking of the heyday of Romanticism, "there was a universal passion for 'genius,' and 'genius' was scarcely thinkable without its external attributes of mystery, suffering, and contempt for the world." Those days have more or less persisted, and so has the interest in Poe. Certain realists of today may demur; they may find little in Poe that has survived from an age of rant and pose and ecstatic gloom. When several years ago Dumas Malone placed Poe fifth on a list of the most important literary figures America has produced, the *Saturday Review of Literature* objected editorially. "Poe," it commented, "is important chiefly as a vested interest of professional scholars . . . hardly anyone would put him on such a list, hardly anyone would call him, except as a historical figure, a first-

6. Karl Mantzius, *A History of Theatrical Art*, London, 1921, Vol. VI, p. 288.

A Prepubescent Style

That Poe had a powerful intellect is undeniable: but it seems to me the intellect of a highly gifted young person before puberty. The forms which his lively curiosity takes are those in which a pre-adolescent mentality delights: wonders of nature and of mechanics and of the supernatural, cryptograms and cyphers, puzzles and labyrinths, mechanical chess-players and wild flights of speculation. The variety and ardour of his curiosity delight and dazzle; yet in the end the eccentricity and lack of coherence of his interests tire. There is just that lacking which gives dignity to the mature man: a consistent view of life. An attitude can be mature and consistent, and yet be highly sceptical: but Poe was no sceptic. He appears to yield himself completely to the idea of the moment: the effect is, that all of his ideas seem to be *entertained* rather than believed. What is lacking is not brain power, but that maturity of intellect which comes only with the maturing of the man as a whole, the development and coordination of his various emotions. I am not concerned with any possible psychological or pathological explanation: it is enough for my purpose to record that the work of Poe is such as I should expect of a man of very exceptional mind and sensibility, whose emotional development has been in some respect arrested at an early age.

T.S. Eliot, *The Hudson Review*, 2, (1949).

rater."[7] The "hardly anyone" is easily debatable. That he is far from being merely a historical figure the preceding pages, I hope, have helped to prove. And if it is true, as the editorial statement admits, that Poe "has been more widely and more exhaustively studied than any other American writer" it has not been so much because he is a vested interest of the scholar as because he is still a living American writer whose power and influence have grown rather than diminished with the passing of time. . . .

It is true that Poe "appealed to sentimental women by his figure, his history and his actions, and to kind-hearted women by his suffering"[8] and that, as Arthur Hopkins once remarked, he has had more posthumous sweethearts than any other American writer.[9] But it is also true that Poe "has

---

7. *Saturday Review of Literature*, April 3, 1937.   8. "The Satanic Streak in Poe's Genius," *Current Literature*, XLVIII, p. 93.   9. The remark was made at a party in Baltimore after the opening of Sophie Treadwell's play, *Plumes in the Dust.* The play failed, like all the plays thus far written on the life of Poe.

furnished mysteries enough for two generations of essayists and biographers, not to list romancers."[10] Three generations is now more exact—and many of the essayists and biographers have been men of sound intellectual astuteness.

It is, as a matter of fact, the work of these men—and of a few women, too—with its painstaking scholarship animated by eagerness to understand and clarify—that has made it possible for Poe to emerge finally neither as a demon nor as a saint, but as a comprehensible human being who happened to be, within his limited field, a great artist. The key to his humanity as well as artistry seems to have been his talent for acting.

Mrs. [Susan Archer] Weiss noted that in "all Poe's accounts of himself, and especially of his feelings, is a palpable affectation and exaggeration, with an extravagance of expression bordering on the tragic and melo-dramatic: a style which is exemplified in some of his writings, and may be equally imaginative in both cases."[11] The applicability of his style to both his emotional life and his artistic creation is not a coincidence. The actor in dress and manner, in love and despair, in school, editorial office, and drawing-room, was also the writer creating parts for the declaimer and handsome, mysterious sufferer. Bishop Fitzgerald remembered him as "distingué in a peculiar sense—a man bearing the stamp of genius and the charm of a melancholy that drew one toward him with a strange sympathy."[12] And that was precisely the rôle Poe had selected for himself. That he was supremely successful in this chosen rôle is evidenced by the almost universal impression he produced, an impression carefully intended and achieved.

The autobiographic nature of much of Poe's writing needs no elaborate proof at this time. His "heroes" are so often portraits of himself that one is justified in comparing the original with them. Roderick Usher, it has already been mentioned, strikingly resembles Poe; William Wilson is undeniably Poe—or as much of him as Stevenson's Mr. Hyde is of Dr. Jekyll or O'Neill's "Loving" is of John Loving (in *Days Without End*). Harrison noted long ago that in "Eleonora" Poe drew "his own silhouette out of the cloudland of memory and self-analysis." It is the silhouette of a dreamer, poet,

10. James S. Wilson, *Virginia Quarterly Review*, II, p. 238.   11. Susan Archer Weiss, *The Home Life of Poe*, New York, 1907, p. 132.   12. *Works*, I, p. 316.

madman; an "ardent lover, the remnant of an ancient race, feverishly enamored of the Beautiful," a "solitary deluged with poetic visions...."[13] Much of all this he undoubtedly was; much of it he believed that he was; all of it he wished others to believe that he was....

For the most part,... he refused to be interested in problems that, according to his aesthetic creed, did not concern the artist. Had he allowed himself to be tainted by the "curse" of didacticism his range might have been wider and his life less self-centered. Professor [Vernon Louis] Parrington's conclusion that "Aside from his art he had no philosophy and no programs and no causes"[14] is, in the main, justified, if we add the word "social" before "philosophy." Poe's art was intensely personal, centripetal; his intellect played upon a cosmos whose core was Edgar Allan Poe. Mallarmé's belief that Poe was killed by a soulless, unimaginative public, the "rabble," is but a blind worshipper's belief. For the truth is that no one killed Poe. He functioned well enough as the human being and writer that he was by heredity, environmental conditioning, education, and the general circumstances of his life. Norms of success differ, but since Poe himself attached so much importance to fame—and yearned passionately for it— is it possible not to conclude that his brief hour upon the stage was reasonably successful? Even Parrington, whose general attitude toward Poe is not overly friendly, is obliged to record that "as an aesthete and a craftsman he made a stir in the world that has not lessened in the years since his death, but has steadily widened."[15] And it was as an aesthete and craftsman that Poe wished to be known, although, like many another person, he also thought himself a monstrously clever fellow in other respects: as a philosopher, for instance; and as a mathematician, and as a generally erudite gentleman.

But the weakness of exhibiting versatility and cleverness, universal as it is, assumes an intense coloring in the actor, and becomes a strength. Poe *was* good at mathematical deductions; his show of erudition *did* impress people; and even his philosophical speculations, such as those so loudly proclaimed in *Eureka*, combined as they were with a strain of poetry, added to his attractiveness. If his acting enveloped him in a sort of solitude, as though he were always on the

13. *Works*, I, p. 132.   14. Vernon Louis Parrington, *The Romantic Revolution in America, 1800–1860*, p. 59.   15. *The Romantic Revolution*, p. 59.

other side of the footlights, behind a proscenium, he nevertheless enjoyed being on display, and he enjoyed the very aura of aloofness. To be sure, psychologically, there may have been another reason for his intrenching himself behind a proscenium. One who does not feel too secure in the midst of a confident self-assured society finds in isolation, in distance, a measure of protection. The principal reason, however, remains: he enjoyed both his isolation and the elevated platform.

Very likely he was often lonely up there on the boards of the world. Behind the actor's mask was the face of a hurt little boy who craved understanding and sympathy and warmth. He found all three in his dear "Muddie," the simple, uncritical Mrs. Clemm, and in "Sissie," his girl wife. Now and then he also found it in one or another of the numerous sentimental ladies who were attracted to him. Mostly, however, women loved him—as Margaret Fuller, writing to Mrs. Browning, remarked—more "with passionate illusion which he amused himself by inducing than with sympathy."[16] This is acute, except that "amused himself" is much too light a phrase for Poe's need to be loved.

That he has greatly "amused" us, for over a century, is the one important fact. A critic of the type of W.C. Brownell may have been temperamentally incapable of doing full justice to a writer like Poe, but he was right in attributing the growth of Poe's legend to "largely romantic" reasons. Some of these reasons have been within us rather than the poet, but the center of all of them has nevertheless been a romantic personality endowed with indubitable gifts and able, like all good actors, to exhibit them arrestingly. This offspring of stage performers was richly equipped to continue their tradition. He was denied the opportunity of following their profession, but he could not help practicing their art. Handsome in face, figure, and bearing, the possessor of a melodious voice and a volatile, sensitive temperament, he also received an education and training which enhanced and refined his natural gifts. He was early taught dancing, drawing, recitation, oratory, and music, everyone of which arts he practiced for his own amusement and that of his friends and public. Besides being of use to him in the drawing-room, they also, especially drawing, music, and oratory, profoundly, affected his writing.

16. Letter from Margaret Fuller to Elizabeth Barrett Browning, December 6, 1849.

WRITING AS ACTING

And that writing was for him as much a form of acting as his public "lectures" or his public challenge to decipher any or all cryptograms. It was also, like all creative art, a form of rich living. Something happened to Edgar Poe when he knew that eyes were upon him, something akin to what happened to Henry James's nobleman who functioned creatively only in public. Poe, to be sure, also had a "private life," but even at his writing table the consciousness of an audience is ever present, and influences the rhythms and patterns, the very idiom and intonation of his work. For, essentially, the one great quality Poe brought to his life and art is the peculiar histrionic ambivalence to feel vicarious experience as though it were his own and to feel his own experience as though it were vicarious. That sense of "dream within a dream" is not mysticism but part of the actor's aloofness from the rôle which fascinates him, an aloofness which enables him to recreate that fascination for the benefit of others.

A lady poet like Mrs. Whitman remembered Poe's

Unfathomable eyes that held the sorrow
Of vanished ages in their shadowy deeps,[17]

but a leading representative of the acting profession understood him more profoundly. On May 4, 1885, a monument to Poe was unveiled at the Metropolitan Museum of Fine Arts in New York. It was Richard Henry Park's "Angel of Sorrow." Among the speakers at the ceremony was Edwin Booth, great romantic actor himself, and son of Junius Brutus Booth, who had once been Poe's boon companion. "The stage," said Edwin Booth in tribute to Poe, "will always live in him as one of her children. The gypsy blood that runs in her veins ran also in his veins, and in the exuberance of his imagination she sees the power and the freedom of her own wild spirit."[18] Booth's prophecy has been fulfilled: the stage still lives in its strange poet-offspring. For, in the final analysis, it is the histrionic quality of Poe's exuberance of imagination which explains his contemporaries and posterity alike.

17. Eugene L. Didier, *The Poe Cult and Other Papers*, New York, 1909, p. 192.
18. William Winter, *Life and Art of Edwin Booth*, p. 281.

Poe as Literary Critic

Edd Winfield Parks

More than a writer and poet, Edgar Allan Poe also
wrote critical literary reviews. According to critic
Edd Winfield Parks, the reviews and magazine
articles that Poe wrote improved his other writing.
A Fulbright lecturer, Parks received the Lamar
Lecture Endowment for his scholarship in culture,
history, and literature and is the author of novels
and poetry as well as scholarly books and articles,
including *Edgar Allan Poe as Literary Critic*, from
which this essay is excerpted.

Edgar Allan Poe was the first important critic to develop and
to refine his critical theories through the media of book reviews and magazine articles. Despite the commonly held
idea that he lived "out of space, out of time," Poe's reputation
in his own day was mainly established by his reviews of contemporary books; he referred to himself as "essentially a
magazinist"; his chief ambition was to own and edit a magazine that would publish, along with stories, poems, and
general articles, an "absolutely independent criticism." At a
time when many writers thought that magazines were
exerting a harmful influence on literature, Poe consistently
defended them:

> The increase, within a few years, of the magazine literature is
> by no means to be regarded as indicating what some critics
> would suppose it to indicate—a downward tendency in
> American taste or in American letters. It is but a sign of the
> times—an indication of an era in which men are forced upon
> the curt, the condensed, the well-digested—in place of the vo-
> luminous. . . . I will not be sure that men at present think
> more profoundly than half a century ago, but beyond ques-
> tion they think with more rapidity, with more skill, with
> more tact, with more of method, and less of excrescence in
> the thought. Besides all this, they have a vast increase in the
> thinking material. They have more facts, more to think about.
> For this reason, they are disposed to put the greatest amount
> of thought in the smallest compass.

FINDING A DIVINE SYSTEM

His innate liking for a literature suitable for magazine publication is one key to Poe's critical theory, A second one, which fitted hand-in-glove with the first, was his search for an ideal unity in literature, similar to the perfect unity of the universe. The natural world, it seemed to him, is governed by a divine system of adaptation in which the beginning leads inevitably to the end, in which means are exactly proportioned to the task to be accomplished, and in which the force expended is precisely proportioned to the work to be done. He sought for the same perfection of form and design in literature, in his own creative work and in the work of others. This desire for a perfect wholeness motivated his dislike for the didactic element in literature: the whole story or poem should be the communication between writer and reader; if the work were rightly done, the effect would be properly secured by the total work, and not by underlining its message or its conclusion.

Poe's old-fashioned use of one word tends to mislead modern readers. He speaks constantly of *plot* and writes many times, with only slight variation and with consistent use of the key word, that "a plot is perfect only inasmuch as we shall find ourselves unable to detach from it or disarrange any single incident involved, without ruin to the whole." Today we are suspicious of plot because it seems to arrange life too artificially. But in our critical thinking we have narrowed the term which Poe so frequently employed. He thought of it as the design, and he saw an analogy between it and the natural world. He desired a whole harmoniously complete in all its parts, a miniature universe which would be comparable to the real universe in which the beginning, middle, and end were held together by an exact and mathematically conceived unity. In the ideal literary design, the end was inevitably foreshadowed and fixed by the beginning; incidents, as middle or means, had to be precisely adjusted to the desired end.

Poe found few books that fitted his stringent theories. As a working critic, he praised many books that only partially achieved what he ideally demanded. But he had a consistent critical theory by which to judge books, although his criteria changed somewhat as he developed. He began in 1831 by placing almost all the creative and the critical faculty in the imagination; by 1835, when he began reviewing books

A REVIEW OF HAWTHORNE'S *TWICE-TOLD TALES*

In this excerpt taken from Poe's critical review of Twice-Told Tales, *Poe (ironically) criticizes Hawthorne for his heavy-handed use of allegory.*

The "peculiarity" or sameness, or monotone of Hawthorne, would, in its mere character of "peculiarity," and without reference to what is the peculiarity, suffice to deprive him of all chance of popular appreciation. But at his failure to be appreciated, we can, *of course,* no longer wonder, when we find him monotonous at decidedly the worst of all possible points—at that point which, having the least concern with Nature, is the farthest removed from the popular intellect, from the popular sentiment and from the popular taste. I allude to the strain of allegory which completely overwhelms the greater number of his subjects, and which in some measure interferes with the direct conduct of absolutely all.

In defence of allegory, (however, or for whatever object, employed,) there is scarcely one respectable word to be said. Its best appeals are made to the fancy—that is to say, to our sense of adaptation, not of matters proper, but of matters improper for the purpose, of the real with the unreal; having never more of intelligible connection than has something with nothing, never half so much of effective affinity as has the substance for the shadow. The deepest emotion aroused within us by the happiest allegory, *as* allegory, is a very, very imperfectly satisfied sense of the writer's ingenuity in overcoming a difficulty we should have preferred his not having attempted to overcome. The fallacy of the idea that allegory, in any of its moods, can be made to enforce a truth—that metaphor, for example, may illustrate as well as embellish an argument—could be promptly demonstrated: the converse of the supposed fact might be shown, indeed, with very little trouble—but these are topics foreign to my present purpose. One thing is clear, that if allegory ever establishes a fact, it is by dint of overturning a fiction. Where the suggested meaning runs through the obvious one in a very profound undercurrent so as never to interfere with the upper one without our own volition, so as never to show itself unless *called* to the surface, there only, for the proper uses of fictitious narrative, is it available at all. Under the best circumstances, it must always interfere with that unity of effect which to the artist, is worth all the allegory in the world. Its vital injury, however, is rendered to the most vitally important point in fiction—that of earnestness or verisimilitude.

regularly for the *Southern Literary Messenger*, he was convinced that reason was equally important, and he made an intensive study of the interplay of reason and imagination. He gradually worked out a theory that imagination or inspiration represented the poetic sentiment, which he also described by such terms as poesy [poetic inspiration], ideality, and the sense of the sublime. But the poem was the means by which a poet brought to the reader a sense of the beautiful, a sense of exaltation; and the completed poem was a product of the reason.

MARRYING INTELLECT TO IMAGINATION

The final stage in his critical development reveals Poe's insistence on the equality of the two forces. With imagination and with reason, "both alike infinite and both alike indestructible," the poet could create a completely unified work if each co-operating faculty exactly equalled the other. This blending of powers he described usually by the term "combining"; he also referred to it as the poetic intellect and the analytic imagination. A poet who lacked this combining force could not possibly produce a unified work.

It was a high, possibly an inhuman, ideal which Poe constantly softened and qualified in his judgments of older and of contemporary poets. He praised Andrew Marvell for achieving it, and praised Longfellow mildly for having partially achieved that goal. His highest praise, significantly, went to Nathaniel Hawthorne for his successful blending of imagination and reason in the field of the short story. Hawthorne had secured unity of effect, totality of impression, intensity, and a sense of ultimate truth in his tales. At his best, he had welded content and form into a perfect whole. Few other writers had succeeded in doing this—so few, in Poe's judgment, that to his contemporaries he seemed to deserve the title of the "tomahawk critic." Yet he seems to have erred more frequently on the side of kindness than of harshness.

He was willing to admit that the building up of a harmonious whole, in prose or in verse, was exceedingly difficult. Not many men could achieve the ultimate function of poetry: the rhythmical creation of beauty. That required a sense of physical or earthly beauty, a sense of spiritual beauty, and a sense of the suggestive power of music. Neither writer nor reader could long sustain the intensity and exaltation of supernal beauty. If the poet is to convey a unified impression of a haunting, indefinite, perfect beauty, he must severely restrict the length of his poem. If the prose writer is to secure a more factual but equally unified sense of reality, he also must limit the scope of his work.

CRITICISM OF A CRITIC

Known for his biting criticism of America's literati, Edgar Allan Poe made enemies. Thomas Dunn English described Poe in his "Notes About Men of Note," which appeared in the Aristidean *in April 1845. In 1846 a quarrel between the formerly friendly colleagues, played out in the press, led to a successful libel suit brought by Poe against English's publisher.*

Edgar A. Poe, one of the editors of the *Broadway Journal.* He never rests. There is a small steam engine in his brain, which not only sets the cerebral mass in motion, but keeps the owner in hot water. His face is a fine one and well-gifted with intellectual beauty. Ideality, with the power of analysis, is shown in his very broad, high and massive forehead—a forehead which would have delighted GALL beyond measure. He would have made a capital lawyer—not a very good advocate, perhaps, but a famous unraveller of all subtleties. He can thread his way through a labyrinth of absurdities, and pick out the sound thread of sense from the tangled skein with which it is connected. He means to be candid, and labours under the strange hallucination that he is so; but he has strong prejudices, and without the least intention of irreverence, would wage war with the DEITY, if the divine canons militated against his notions. His sarcasm is subtle and searching. He can do nothing in the common way; and buttons his coat after a fashion peculiarly his own. If we ever caught him doing a thing like anybody else, or found him reading a book any other way than upside down, we would implore his friends to send for a straight jacket, and a Bedlam doctor. He were mad, then, to a certainty.

Thomas Dunn English, from "Notes About Men of Note" from *Aristidean*, April 1845.

It has been noted frequently that Poe's critical theories and his creative talents complement each other with amazing exactitude. Some later scholars have attempted to prove that the theories are only rationalizations of Poe's own creative limitations. This is undoubtedly true to the extent that he believed an author should be fully aware of the capabilities of the art that he practiced: in his own work and in his judgment of others, he held firmly to his central conception that art was not a spontaneous overflow of genius, but a designed effect.

A NARROW FIELD

The literary field that Poe tilled was undeniably narrow. He lacked breadth of vision, broad human sympathy, and a warmhearted comprehension of many diverse types of people. For these he substituted intensity of thought and emotion, and a tight perfection of form. His theories likewise unduly narrow the field of literature, especially of poetry. He would rule out of that domain the major works of writers like Dante, Milton, and Goethe. But his positive accomplishments were definite, and widely influential. Nowhere were they more far-reaching than in the field of criticism. At a time when romantic writers were talking of self-expression, he concentrated not on the artist but on the created work of art. It was from Poe's logical formulas for a poem that Baudelaire and the French symbolists (especially Mallarmé and, much later, Valéry) derived their form, their doctrine of the interpenetration of the senses, and their idea of an allusive, indefinite imagery and rhythm that would have the suggestiveness of music. It was from Poe's essays on form (especially "The Poetic Principle" and "The Philosophy of Composition") that Gautier and the Parnassians derived much of their philosophy that the form creates the idea.

Poe's final value as a critic can hardly be judged apart from his influence on the French poets, and it was through them that he has influenced such modern American poets as T.S. Eliot and Wallace Stevens. To his contemporaries and to the immediately following generations in America, he seemed in this respect outside the main currents of American thought. But if this influence has come back to us indirectly, through Europe, another phase of his critical work had and continues to have a direct bearing on our thought. He emphasized compression, brevity, unity of effect; he set the highest value on literary types more suitable for magazines than for books. More than any other critic, Poe developed a tenable aesthetic for a magazine age.

Chapter 2

Poe's Themes

Symbolism in Poe's Tales

Georges Zayed

In this essay excerpted from his book *The Genius of Edgar Allan Poe*, Georges Zayed describes Poe's use of symbolism in his short tales. Zayed describes the symbolism in scenes from many of Poe's most well known tales to identify the major themes in Poe's works.

The world of Edgar Allan Poe with its abnormalities, its queerness, and its monstrosities, appears at first sight completely alien to our world, as well as to the American milieu of Poe's time. It is all the more astonishing because the young America of that time had barely come to life and was breathing deeply of youth, health and vigor. Undoubtedly the creation of a world set apart, imaginary and timeless, conferred upon Poe's stories a universal character and a transcendence which corresponded to an internal reality, detached from contingencies, and consequently eternal. At the same time, it reflected perfectly the principles upon which his literary doctrine was founded: on the one hand, the knowledge of the objectivity of the work of art and its independence of all personal, moral, utilitarian or realistic preoccupation; and on the other, the obligation of the artist to make his works a product of pure imagination with the aim of transporting us into the realm of dreams and supraterrestrial Beauty. Seen from this point of view, this universe which seems so alien to ours appears, after analysis, closer than one might have thought, for in reality it is within us, in our own hearts and senses, and is their metaphorical expression.

Everything in effect is clarified in this work, even the situations which are most paradoxical, and the characters which are the most aberrant, if one looks upon them as sym-

Excerpted from *The Genius of Edgar Allan Poe* by Georges Zayed. Copyright ©1985 by Schenkman Publishing Company, Inc. Reprinted by permission of the publisher.

bols rather than taking the story literally: symbols of what is hidden, secret, even unavowable, repugnant or tragic, within us. Everything appears plausible if one considers them not as the manifestations of an individual consciousness (that of Poe), but as the concrete rendering of states of mind common to everyone, and visions born in our imagination or buried in the depths of our subconscious. In this way one can rediscover the human being more clearly in his complexity as well as in his unity. Half of Poe's stories (and poems)—if not all of them—are in effect symbolic; they bear a hidden sense which is sometimes difficult to penetrate. A symbolist interpretation reveals the profound significance of works which would otherwise leave us perplexed, surprised or outraged. . . .

To examine Poe's entire symbolic world in a few pages is, of course, out of the question. Let it suffice here to register a few typical examples. . . .

THE HUMAN CONDITION AS A PRISON

To show that the human condition is a sort of prison where man is locked within his physical shell from which he can only escape through death—or in dreams by imagination— Poe has recourse to a number of symbols: "The Pit and the Pendulum," "MS. Found in a Bottle," "A Descent in the Maelström," etc. Man's struggle to liberate himself is expressed by intense activity on the part of the hero, changes in place, voyages, flights. The many adventures in Poe's stories reflect a morbid psychological instability and underline man's anxiety in his abandonment, his existential anguish, and the keen longing of the soul for escape. All this activity moreover comes to a dead end, in fact to death itself, after an unpredictable period of suspense—even if the heroes momentarily succeed in escaping uninjured.

In the first of these stories, "The Pit and the Pendulum," Poe emphasizes the futility of these desperate and impotent efforts; salvation can only come from outside. The dungeon of the Inquisition is the imaginary representation of the human condition, a prison where our acts are under surveillance, recorded, judged and punished. The wretched man, knocked on his back in the shadows and strapped down on a wooden framework on the edge of a pit full of putrid vapors: this is the human being condemned to the pangs of life from which he can only escape by falling into nothingness (the pit). The heavy pendulum whose tip is sharp as a razor balances itself by coming closer and closer to the neck of the prisoner just as the walls narrow in on him: this is the inevitable course of life, the destructive force of Time which overcomes us. In this frightful situation, salvation can only come from on high. Poe, in this story, simultaneously takes up the problem of dreams and waking, of the disintegration of the personality and the loss of identity.

In the "MS. Found in a Bottle," there is a separation between the perishable physical shell and the immortal and divine spirit (the monarch "Thought" of the "Haunted Palace") which is all that counts; the body can disappear without loss, the spirit always remains, through its manifestations, for it is a ray of divine light and a particle of the celestial soul. But the boat in the story is ever the image of life, fleeing at a giddy speed toward its destiny which is the fall into the abyss and into nothingness. And the protagonist, a solitary voyager who passes through a world of strangers, worried and aged and indifferent to him, this is the image of man—of modern man—a prisoner in his solitude, his anguish and his misery: "We are surely doomed to hover continually upon the brink of Eternity, without taking a final plunge into the abyss." Nevertheless, there is something heroic in his attitude and his refusal to let himself fall into despair. He knows that life is a unique experience and that there is something irreplaceable about it which is worthwhile saving even at the price of his own being: "It is evident that we are hurrying onwards to some exciting knowledge—some never-to-be-imparted secret, whose attainment is destruction.". . .

It is the same in *The Narrative of A. Gordon Pym,* which is Poe's most important work—at least by its length. The swell of the sea, the storm and the surf symbolize movements produced by the emotions in the labyrinth of consciousness, and irrational swirls of the unconscious in the "subterranean world of darkness," which are treated in "The Pit and the Pendulum." At the same time they refer to the instability of human life and the precariousness of its moving universe. In "The Gold Bug," once again, but in a completely different sphere, it is the victory of thought, reflection and lucidity which reveals the hidden rationality underlying the behaviour of madness. Contrary to all logical expectations, Mr. Legrand deciphers a cryptogram which leads him to the discovery of a fabulous treasure.

THE SYNTHETIC STORIES

Thus every time reason prevails over unconscious forces, the hero finds salvation; in the opposite case, if it loses control and irrational forces carry the day, he is doomed to madness or death or both. That is what differentiates the preceding "analytic" stories, realistic in their minute study of sensations and in which the safeguard of identity is assured, from the "synthetic" stories, like "The Fall of the House of Usher"... or "The Black Cat," where a delirious imagination corrupts the data of the senses, distorts the reality and unhinges the mind of the heroes: there we witness the disintegration of the being and the loss of identity by dissociation between senses and conscience. The final fall into the abyss or nothingness by madness or death is the normal end of this process.

This is what we find in "The Fall of the House of Usher" in which Usher says: "I *must* perish in this deplorable folly. ... I feel that the period will sooner or later arrive when I must abandon life and reason together, in some struggle with the grim phantasm, FEAR." This tale is the most authentic expression of Poe's symbolism: it accentuates the mysteries of the unconscious life and the irrational progression of obsessions; it provokes terror and results in the insanity of the protagonist; moreover, the author makes constant use of correspondences. The analogy is, in effect, complete between the shattered mental state of Roderick Usher, shaken by abnormal terrors and wasted away by dismal obsessions, and the desolation of his surroundings. Poe refers to "the original title of the estate in the quaint and equivocal appellation of the "House of Usher"—an appellation which seemed to include, in the mind of the peasantry who used it, both the family and the family mansion." The old house with its "fissure" going from the roof to the foundation, its "bleak" walls, its "crumbling" stones, its "vacant and eye-like" windows, its "tattered" furnishings, its somber tapestries through which filter the "feeble gleams of encrimsoned light," the "ebon blackness" of the floors, the "fantasmagoric armorial trophies," all this reflects the maze of consciousness threatened by insanity, "the subterranean world of darkness." Nature and the surrounding atmosphere correspond no less to the state of mind of Usher: the "singularly dreary" country, the "black and lurid tarn." The weather also adds to this desolation: "a dull, dark, and soundless day in the autumn," where the clouds hang "oppressively low" in the sky. All gives rise to "a sense of insufferable gloom," an "atmosphere of sorrow," an "air of stern, deep, and irredeemable" melancholy. "The Fall of the House of Usher" is a symbol for that world which crawls and creeps in the depths of being.

Nothing is more typical of this symbolism than the poem included in the story entitled "The Haunted Palace," a long allegory (somewhat hyperbolic) of visions which the imagination calls forth in the "enchanted" realm of dreams, beyond the borders of reality. It is also the image of the human condition: happiness cannot last; griefs and afflictions take over. From another point of view (for the sometimes esoteric symbolism of Poe can have more than one interpretation), it is the personification of the harmonious ordering of ideas by lucid Reason, surrendering to the assault of the irrational forces which obfuscate it. For Poe himself, as he admitted in a letter, it represents "a mind haunted by phantoms.". . .

THE STRUGGLE AGAINST NOTHINGNESS

"Ligeia," although it represents the division of the ego, the split personality, the conflict between irrational forces and reason powerless to preserve the integrity of the self and the identity of the protagonist, shows the power of thought over nothingness, and of the will struggling against death. In addition to the sado-masochist obsessions and hallucinations which lead the hero to persecuting madness and to crime (did he not practically assassinate Rowena by submitting her to an atrocious and insane treatment, not to mention the poison which he administered to her), "Ligeia" translates the aspirations of the poet towards an ideal of supraterrestrial beauty, incarnate in a woman: "the beauty of beings either above or apart from the earth," "the triumph of all things heavenly." It relates "the experience of a man who has known the illumination of Beauty and who, once he has lost it, strives to find it again." His marriage with Rowena, which he considers a "profanation," actually means "an alliance with reality."

We discover the same symbolism in "Metzengerstein," which is the incarnation of the spirit of evil and triumphant madness receiving their chastisement by fire. The fire in the castle, and the death of the young, debauched and cruel Count in the flames represent the disintegration of the personality and the breaking up of the intelligence governed by irrational forces. Stephen Mooney rather thinks that "Metzengerstein," like "Usher" is a "parable of Gothic." "Each tale is a family, a castle, a display of human perversity, and a gathering of all these self-destructive forces into their own annihilation . . . [They] are fatal dramas of cognition. The imagination [is] caught up in one symbolic action, a psychoarchitectural or psychosomatic gesture, in which mind and body, dying together, become one."

A Demoniac Undertone

Almost without the first sign of moral principle, or of the concrete or its heroisms, or the simpler affections of the heart, Poe's verses illustrate an intense faculty for technical and abstract beauty, with the rhyming art to excess, an incorrigible propensity toward nocturnal themes, a demoniac undertone behind every page—and, by final judgment, probably belong among the electric lights of imaginative literature, brilliant and dazzling, but with no heat. There is an indescribable magnetism about the poet's life and reminiscences, as well as the poems. To one who could work out their subtle retracing and retrospect, the latter would make a close tally no doubt between the author's birth and antecedents, his childhood and youth, his physique, his so-call'd education, his studies and associates, the literary and social Baltimore, Richmond, Philadelphia and New York of those times—not only the places and circumstances in themselves, but often, very often, in a strange spurning of, and reaction from them all.

Walt Whitman, from *Specimen Days*, entry for January 1, 1880.

Most of the other stories can be interpreted in the same fashion, and with both perspicacity and intuition one can understand their hidden obscure meaning. In the symbol of the balloon, Poe, like a new Hamlet, shows that there are more things between heaven and earth than can meet the eye; and the flying machine of "Hans Pfaal" which lands on the moon is a hoax only in appearance; through the sense of mystery which human intelligence tries to penetrate, it incarnates the triumph of the spirit. We find the same expression of the mysteries surrounding us in "Mesmeric Revelation"—which in certain respects prefigures *Eureka*—and of the more remote and far more formidable mysteries of the beyond. The shadows of doubt that the author, in his thirst of knowledge, wants to dissipate by interrogating a hypnotized dying man about God, the soul, matter, spirit, the future life, good and evil, are but the metaphysical anguish that every human being feels before the idea of what awaits him beyond the grave; and the last sentence of the story reveals its profound significance: "Had the sleep-walker, indeed, during the latter portion of his discourse, been addressing me from out of the region of the shadows?"

In spite of the veritable obsession with nihility [nothingness] which Poe demonstrates and the anguish which accompanies him (at least until *Eureka),* he knows that, so far as matter is concerned, all of our efforts are vain and that sooner or later everything ends by returning into nothingness—or into the great "Whole"—"the vast animate and sentient whole." He realizes that physical beauty as well as the dream of this beauty will also be engulfed. This is what emerges from "The Island of the Fay" (which is an ecstatic dream in the midst of nature more than a tale). The sunny side, "radiant harem of garden beauties," represents life, and the shadowy region of the "ebony" river hides the empire of death; every round trip of the canoe being one year of human life, the cycle of the seasons vanishes into nothingness.

FATE: LIFE AND DEATH

The symbolism of certain stories of Poe is rather clear, and it would be useless to insist upon it. For example, "The Masque of the Red Death" is "a parable of the inevitability and universality of death," "the human condition of man's fate, and the fate of the universe." The seven rooms are none other than the seven ages of man; the gigantic ebony clock with the "dull, heavy, monotonous clang," emphasizes the passage of time; and the spectre in the winding sheet smeared with blood, is the personification of death, or "man's ... self-aroused and self-developed fear of his own mistaken concept of death." In "The Man of the Crowd," the old man clearly allegorizes conscience tormented by remorse, burdened with fear, incapable of remaining face to face with itself in the solitude which terrifies it. It is the same thing in its corollary, "Silence," which expresses "in one solemn vision the necessity we feel to search for self-forgetfulness in the bustling excitement outside ourselves, incapable of bearing the silence of meditation which would condemn us to the spectacle of our own misery." It is also the twists and turns of remorse that "The Tell-Tale Heart" renders in its ever more violent beating—driving the assassin to denounce himself. Even if he appears as "the deranged victim of a hallucinatory nightmare," who fears death and dreads Time symbolized by the old man, he destroys himself by trying to free his sensitivity from this fear. He is "a haunted and bewildered imagination" who refuses "to accept himself as a creature caught in the temporal net." In "William Wilson," it is not much different: the narrator powerless to achieve the unity of his personality and to live in peace with his conscience,—allegorized in a double of himself—struggles with it and tries all his life to repudiate it; he understood too late that, by murdering it, he destroyed a part of his own being.

Beauty and Nature

Certain other stories are the sheer expression of Poe's aesthetic principles. For example "The Oval Portrait" which contrasts reality and art is one of his fundamental literary ideas. In passing through the magic paintbrush of the artist, reality loses its vital characteristics which are transferred into the work of art; or to put it another way, artistic creation, by borrowing its elements from the tangible world, relieves them, so to speak, of their own life and breathes a new life into them.

Finally, Poe makes constant use of the correspondence between the natural setting and the state of mind of his protagonists, as we have seen in "The Fall of the House of Usher." Examples are numerous in all his works and can be found in practically any of his stories. But it is particularly noticeable in two of them, "Morella" and "Eleonora," because it is more deliberate, and also in the "landscape-gardens": "The Elk" [Morning on the Wissahiccon], "The Domain of Arnheim," "Landor Cottage." The latter, from a certain point of view, seems to be paradise lost and found thanks to art and imagination, capable of recreating the golden age in the midst of an ideal nature. In the first of these stories Poe writes in fact: "The vast valley of Louisiana . . . is a realization of the wildest dreams of paradise." But this paradise is threatened by industry, mechanization, and progress. This is why these stories symbolize Poe's regrets for the "good old days," when the "Demon of the Engine" was not, when "picnics" were undreamed of, when "water-privileges" were neither bought nor sold, and when "the red man trod alone, with the elk, upon the ridges." At the same time, these stories are attacks against American utilitarianism, and an argument for the return to nature, to primitive innocence, where the harmony between man and the milieu was assured. . . .

THE PSYCHOLOGICAL STORIES

In the psychological stories the landscape is different: it is a state of mind. Nature vibrates and reacts in harmony with human soul. In "Morella," the serenity of the heroine in the face of death is expressed by a calm and peaceful decor: "The winds lay still in heaven. . . . There was a dim mist over all the earth, and a warm glow upon the waters, and, amid the rich October leaves of the forest, a rainbow from the firmament had surely fallen." After her death occurs a change in interior and exterior decor: "the heaven of this pure affection became darkened, and gloom, and horror, and grief, swept over it in clouds. . . . The stars of my fate faded from heaven, and therefore the earth grew dark . . . the winds of the firmament breathed but one sound within my ears, and the ripples upon the sea murmured evermore—Morella."

This intimate fusion of nature and the soul is also very noticeable in "Eleonora"—a true prose poem in its structure and in the emotions which animate it! The same correspondences and the same variations between the real and psychological landscapes are evident. The "Valley of the Many-Colored Grass" symbolizes earthly paradise "carpeted by a soft green grass," "vanilla-perfumed," and besprinkled with all kinds of flowers. It undergoes a first transformation "for the better" in expressing the passion of love, and adds to its beauty new attractive elements: the "gay glowing birds," the "golden and silver fish," and "a lulling melody more divine than that of the harp of Aeolus." A cloud "all gorgeous and crimson and gold" shut the lovers within "a magic prison-house of grandeur and of glory." After the death of Eleonora, nature loses all of its charm in a third change: "the star-shaped flowers shrank"; and "the tints of green carpet faded"; the birds deserted the valley and the fish fled the river; the music ceased and everything returned into its original silence.

One could multiply these examples indefinitely: all of them demonstrate positively that Poe's stories, as a whole, are not mere tales designed to entertain the reader; they are narratives rich in learning which oblige us to reflect upon them in order to extract the "substantive marrow." As he put it himself, the meaning lies not on the surface of the tale—or of the poem—but below it, as dark undercurrent. This symbolism permitted him to confer a human significance upon his themes and to make them representative of our aspirations and our anguishes. They reveal our anxiety about the unknown, the terrors hidden in the depths of our consciousness, and the tragedy of our destiny in the face of the mystery of death and the beyond. If this makes Poe in certain respects the precursor of modern literature, of the literature of the absurd, and existentialism, if moreover he announces a characteristic of the symbolism of Kafka and its nightmarish atmosphere, he nevertheless surpasses these with his confidence in human reason and his faith in the dignity of man, his devotion to art and poetry, as well as his profound love of nature (a particle of divine intelligence). All these traits transcend and purify his pessimism, and open it to a world of unearthly beauty and future hope.

Death in Poe's Writings

J. Gerald Kennedy

Edgar Allan Poe's childhood and adulthood were marred by the death of close relatives. His parents died when he was two, his stepmother when he was twenty, and his young wife also before her time. Given this biographical information, it sometimes puzzles people that Poe wrote about death in such an overly sentimental way. According to J. Gerald Kennedy, Poe wrote about death in an unrealistic, Victorian way because it was a convention of his day—he wanted to sell books—though he did not personally believe in a sentimental or beautiful death. Kennedy examines Poe's poems and stories to show how he used death to evoke a mood and to make certain points in his writing. Kennedy is the author of *Poe, Death, and the Life of Writing*, from which the following is excerpted.

Poe's attraction to the problem of death is so conspicuous that the reticence of modern criticism on the subject seems inexplicable. Here we find a writer whose entire oeuvre is marked by a compulsive interest in the dimensionality of death: its physical signs, the phenomenology of dying, the deathbed scene, the appearance of the corpse, the effects of decomposition, the details of burial, the danger of premature interment, the reanimation of the dead, the lure of tombs and cemeteries, the nature of mourning and loss, the experience of dread, the compulsion to inflict death upon another, and the perverse desire to seek one's own death. Typically these elements have been thought to express an unsound and morbid sensibility, a neurosis rooted in traumatic early experience, a conscious exploitation of Gothic conventions to produce the effect of terror, or an esoteric symbolism for the representation of philosophical or aesthetic concepts.... What criticism has largely overlooked is Poe's relentless ef-

Excerpted from *Poe, Death, and the Life of Writing* by J. Gerald Kennedy. Copyright ©1987 by Yale University. Reprinted by permission of the publisher, Yale University Press.

fort to probe the nature of modern death anxiety.

For Poe the imaginary was dominated by the gigantic presence of death; but death held contradictory meanings, and its tangible image changed through the course of his engagement with writing. . . .

Poe's . . . poetic treatment of dying women indicates that, to a certain extent, he shared the pervasive sentimental view that death intensified female beauty and even brought about a purification of loveliness. Thus for example in "Lenore" he idealized the departed one:

> The sweet Lenore hath gone before, with Hope that flew
>   beside,
> Leaving thee wild for the dear child that should have been
>   thy bride—
> For her, the fair and debonair, that now so lowly lies,
> The life upon her yellow hair, but not within her eyes—
> The life still there upon her hair, the death upon her eyes.

This lyric captures the subtle eroticism of a beauty heightened by the implication that Lenore takes to the grave the charms which she had not yet yielded to her "wild" lover, Guy de Vere. But Poe's emphasis on the death of "innocence" is also consistent with gift-book evocations of the saintly departure. More frequently in his verses, the beauty of the beloved is an obsessive memory; his speakers recall "the rare and radiant maiden whom the angels name Lenore" (in "The Raven") or "the bright eyes/Of the beautiful Annabel Lee." Poe could argue (in "The Philosophy of Composition") that the death of a beautiful woman offered the most poetical subject imaginable because that motif conjoined the essential elements of desire: irresistible loveliness and the impossibility of its preservation or recovery. The ephemerality of such beauty accounted for its force: unlike the timeless beauty of the work of art, the loveliness of Poe's women is doubly evanescent, being both an aspect of youth (which is lost daily) and a symptom of illness (which must end in death). This aesthetic no doubt developed in part from the much-noted irony that consumption—the all-too-common destroyer in the nineteenth century—actually did enhance physical beauty at an intermediate stage by inducing a feverish glow. In Poe's tales, which deal more directly with the *process* of dying, fated women seem invariably to grow more beautiful as they approach their last hour. Poe implies that through this insidious transformation, temporal loveliness approaches the perfection of eternal beauty, and theoretically at least the corpse of the dead woman briefly incarnates an ideality. But because death also entails physiological decay, the beauty of the just-departed contains an element of terror, since the passage of time implies a subsequent and inevitable mutation to loathsomeness. Death discloses its cruel paradoxicality, being both the source of ideal beauty and its destroyer. Poe could accept the perverse fact that death intensified beauty—he had seen it often enough—but he also saw through the illusion fostered by sentimentalism. . . .

THE RELATIONSHIP BETWEEN DEATH AND BEAUTY

In calling poetry the "rhythmical creation of beauty," and then designating the death of a beautiful woman as the most poetical of topics, Poe established an implicit metaphorical relationship between the death of beauty and poetic texts. The poems . . . may be understood as figurations of the problem of beauty, its earthly fate, and its translation through death—first into an ideal form and then into an object of disgust. As such, these poems appear to allegorize for Poe the fate of poetry: the poetic text stands over and against mundane reality and subjects itself to the "death" of publication (separation) and public judgment (corruption). The recurrent tension between heaven and hell and the occasional suggestion that the woman has been destroyed by calumny (as in "Lenore") or victimized by jealous rivals (implied in the final version of "To One in Paradise" and in "Annabel Lee") strengthen one's sense of a relationship between the poem itself and the fated woman who is its subject. Seemingly cursed by her beauty, the dying woman is typically too fine or pure for earthly survival, too ethereal to be appreciated by vulgar contemporaries. The crucial relationship exists between the woman and the speaker—between the work and its author. Poe seems in this way to dramatize the writer's problematic relationship to his own texts. An unwritten poem exists only as a phantasm of the poet's imagination, but once reified as verse, once translated into the language of the tribe, the writing assumes a life of its own, conditioned by the vagaries of reception. For the poet, the essential beauty of the original idea always remains in some sense untranslatable; yet its "body" (which becomes part of the larger corpus) suffers the indignities of scorn, neglect, envy, misunderstanding, and misquotation. . . .

Insofar as Poe associates the woman with beauty and the

poetic sentiment in general, she may be said to incarnate the desire of writing. In an important sense, her power over the writer lies in her otherness or her remoteness; that is, her personal beauty, characterized as a "strangeness," is the physical sign of a difference which is irreducible and inexplicable. Poe says of the poetic sentiment that it is "the desire of the moth for the star," the insatiable longing for the unreachable; likewise the beautiful woman embodies that which compels the writer yet remains unattainable. Writing is a form of nympholepsy. . . .

"LIGEIA"

Ligeia personifies for the narrator a will to live and a loveliness which verges on the "supernal Beauty" of poetry itself. Poe has evoked the woman from his own poetic text, the youthful "Al Aaraaf":

> Ligeia! Ligeia!
>   My beautiful one!
> Whose harshest idea
>   Will to melody run . . .

The fictional text delineates her exquisite strangeness: a "lofty and pale" forehead, skin of "purest ivory, " "raven-black hair, " teeth of "a brilliancy almost startling," and eyes of "the most brilliant of black." Like Berenice and Morella, Ligeia grows ill and takes on the characteristics of mortal decline: "The wild eyes blazed with a too—too glorious effulgence; the pale fingers became of the transparent waxen hue of the grave, and the blue veins upon the lofty forehead swelled and sank impetuously with the tides of the most gentle emotion. I saw that she must die." Before she dies, however, Ligeia delivers herself of a poem, "The Conqueror Worm," which comprises a radical response to consolation literature, positing a grim, naturalistic image of "human gore." Unlike Margaret Davidson, who is said to have died without a struggle or groan, Ligeia listens to the recitation of her poem and then shrieks: "O God! O Divine Father!—shall these things be undeviatingly so?—shall this conqueror be not once conquered?" What Ligeia expresses at this moment is Kierkegaardian "fear and trembling," the characteristic dilemma of the modern age. At the core of this uncertainty is the awareness that despite increasing information and knowledge, the denizen of a secular, technological culture can never entirely surmount what [critic] Becker calls the "horror of his own basic animal condition."

Poe's narrator tells us that he is "crushed into the very dust with sorrow" by Ligeia's death. He voices no expectation of heavenly reunion, but he seizes upon the suggestion of his dying wife that she will return to him through force of will. On the surface, he seems to have participated in her dying moments as the narrator of "Morella" was unable to do, but the second half of the story hints that he too has, in some way, avoided the dying woman, repressed the terror of the transformation, and doomed himself to an inevitable reenactment. In the months after Ligeia's death, he gives himself up to "aimless wandering" and then begins to refurbish an abbey "with a faint hope of alleviating [his] sorrows." But his selection of funereal artifacts (such as the "gigantic sarcophagus of black granite") reveals that, as with the speaker in "The Raven," his effort to forget conceals a stronger urge to remember, to resurrect the departed. He tells us that "in a moment of mental alienation" he has married Rowena, the Anglo-Saxon antithesis of Ligeia, upon whom he projects an irrational hatred rooted presumably in guilt over remarriage (a theme in "Eleonora" as well). As Roy Basler pointed out, the narrator thus cunningly engineers the collapse of Rowena, and the image of his second wife's "pallid and rigid figure upon the bed" brings to mind Ligeia's demise and "the whole of that unutterable wo[e] with which [he] had regarded her thus enshrouded." A deep psychic necessity impels him to reconstruct in this way the final agonies of Ligeia, perhaps as a symptomatic expression of survivor guilt. During this night of the living dead, Rowena's morbid relapses cause two associated effects: the narrator's shudder of horror at "the ghastly expression of death" and his "waking visions of Ligeia." The mingling of past and present pushes him toward the edge of madness; the woman before him is both living and dead, Lady Rowena and Ligeia, an impossible image of desire and loathing.

A FASCINATION WITH A CORPSE

While the narrator's treatment of Rowena may be explained as a symptom of his guilt at taking a second wife, a more disturbing possibility surfaces in his fascination with the woman's "corpse." In this preoccupation he reveals himself to be a connoisseur of decay, attentive to the signs of death, the awful work of translation. The narrator's own questioning of the act of inscription illuminates his compulsion:

> But why shall I minutely detail the unspeakable horrors of that
> night? Why shall I pause to relate how, time after time, until
> near the period of the gray dawn, this hideous drama of reviv-
> ification was repeated; how each terrific relapse was only into
> a sterner and apparently more irredeemable death; how each
> agony wore the aspect of a struggle with some invisible foe;
> and how each struggle was succeeded by I know not what
> wild change in the personal appearance of the corpse?

Why indeed does he devote such close attention to the physical condition of Rowena? Such detail of course prepares the
reader for the final scene in which the two women merge.
But the narrator's scrutiny of the "hideous drama of revivification" reveals a peculiar interest in physiological change,

MAKING THE IMAGINARY REAL

*Unlike W.B. Yeats, Russian novelist Fyodor Dostoyevsky
thought highly of Poe's work, especially his ability to make
fantastic details seem unusually real. This comment is part of a
review of Poe's work that appeared in the Russian newspaper*
Wremia, *or* Time. *It was translated by Vladimir Astrov.*

Not fantastic should [Poe] be called but capricious. And how
odd are the vagaries of his fancy and at the same time how
audacious! He chooses as a rule the most extravagant reality,
places his hero in a most extraordinary outward or psychological situation, and, then, describes the inner state of that person with marvellous acumen and amazing realism. Moreover,
there exists one characteristic that is singularly peculiar to
Poe and which distinguishes him from every other writer, and
that is the vigor of his imagination. Not that his fancy exceeds
that of all other poets, but his imagination is endowed with a
quality which in such magnitude we have not met anywhere
else, namely the power of details. Try, for instance, yourselves
to realize in your mind anything that is very unusual or has
never before occurred, and is only conceived as possible, and
you will experience how vague and shadowy an image will
appear before your inner eye. You will either grasp more or
less general traits of the inward image or you will concentrate
upon the one or the other particular, fragmentary feature. Yet
Edgar Poe presents the whole fancied picture or events in all
its details with such stupendous plasticity that you cannot but
believe in the reality or possibility of a fact which actually
never has occurred and even never could happen.

Fyodor M. Dostoyevsky, "Three Tales of Edgar Poe," from *Wremia*, 1861.

here encountered as the dreamlike repetition of a surreal back-and-forth movement between health and corruption. The narrator experiences a compressed version of all of the declines witnessed by his counterparts in other tales. He describes himself (on the night of his vigil) as paralyzed by "unutterable horror and awe, for which the language of mortality has no sufficiently energetic expression," and yet the text itself betrays an obstinate curiosity about the object of this "horror and awe" and a determination to represent its nature through a system of signs already declared to be inadequate.

What impels him to write is the tacit sense that Rowena's ambiguous condition, her wavering between resurrection and decomposition, expresses both the paradoxical mockery of death and the uncertainty of his own response to its transformation. Though he acknowledges a disgust for his "fair-haired and blue-eyed" second wife, arranges the "bridal chamber" to exacerbate the "nervous irritation of her temperament," and expresses no grief at her apparent demise, he twice makes an unlikely effort to revive her. In the first instance he speaks of his "endeavors to call back the spirit still hovering" and at her second recovery he affirms: "The lady *lived;* and with redoubled ardor I betook myself to the task of restoration. I chafed and bathed the temples and the hands, and used every exertion which experience, and no little medical reading, could suggest." We should probably attribute these efforts not to solicitude but to voyeuristic interest in the cycle of corruption. Each time the woman stirs, she relapses into a more frightful condition; after a first flush of life, "the color disappeared from both eyelid and cheek, leaving a wanness even more than that of marble; the lips became doubly shrivelled and pinched up in the ghastly expression of death; a repulsive clamminess and coldness overspread rapidly the surface of the body; and all the usual rigorous stiffness immediately supervened." At her second relapse, "the color fled, the pulsation ceased, the lips resumed the expression of the dead, and, in an instant afterward, the whole body took upon itself the icy chilliness, the livid hue, the intense rigidity, the sunken outline, and all the loathsome peculiarities of that which has been, for many days, a tenant of the tomb." "Time after time" the same experience repeats itself, as the spellbound narrator finds himself the "helpless prey to a whirl of violent emotions."

The meaning of the scene is complex, for on one level it

exposes a cultural and historical anxiety: divested of sentimental illusion, the dead body has become a potentially re-
volting sight. Yet the memory of a beautiful woman's death
superimposes itself upon the narrator's perception of the
body's metamorphosis. The "drama of revivification" is
"hideous" yet utterly absorbing; and its interest seems to lie
in its radical indeterminacy. Rowena is neither living nor
dead; she incarnates the indefinable, the anomalous. The
seeming reversibility of her condition enables the narrator
to contemplate that which can ordinarily be glimpsed only
as a transitional moment, as a liminal state—the marginal-
ity upon which Poe bases the poetics of translation. If the
death of a beautiful woman is "the most poetical topic in the
world," its aesthetic value derives neither from female
beauty as such nor from death as an ontological event, but
from the unstable relation between the two, from the shifting intermediacy of a phenomenon which has no proper
place or form or intelligibility. The narrator has witnessed
this process before, when its unfolding deprived him of
Ligeia; now he examines the back-and-forth movement in-
tently, for in his own contradictory response of horror and
fascination he confronts the dilemma of translation. The
"language of mortality" has no equivalent word for a transformation of this kind, no means of articulating the in-
between nature of dying. . . .

DEATH AS A PARADOX

For Poe, the death of a beautiful woman posed in absolute
terms the paradox of our creaturely condition. The beauty of
woman seemed a sign of the eternal, an apparent proof of
paradise and immortality. Yet disease transformed beauty
into a ghastly parody of itself, turning desire to loathing and
love to disgust. The dying woman became a sign of her own
fate, and her dissolution presented a spectacle at once irresistible and unbearable. In the relation of the narrator to the
beloved, Poe staged the inevitable conflict between mind and
flesh, between the longing for "Supernal Beauty" and the
threat of cessation. Female loveliness manifested for Poe the
essence of poetry:

> He feels it in the beauty of woman—in the grace of her step—
> in the lustre of her eye—in the melody of her voice—in her
> soft laughter—in her sigh—in the harmony of the rustling of
> her robes. He deeply feels it in her winning endearments—in

> her burning enthusiasms—in her gentle charities—in her
> meek and devotional endurances—but above all—ah, far
> above all—he kneels to it—he worships it in the faith, in the
> purity, in the strength, in the altogether divine majesty—of
> her *love.*

Yet the eternality of female beauty could not withstand con-
tamination by reality. Only in poetry, in a work of art—an
oval portrait, perhaps—could loveliness escape the "vermin
fangs" of the Conqueror Worm. For the beautiful woman was
(like Ulalume) destined to become a "dread burden"; she
was (like Lenore) always "doubly dead" in that her death
marked the end of a particular life and the collapse of that
myth of immortality which her beauty seemed to guarantee.
Her apparent return from the grave in "Morella," "Ligeia,"
and "Usher" dramatizes the contradictory desires of memory and forgetfulness experienced by the narrator of "The
Raven": the beautiful woman cannot be buried, for the monstrous irony which she incarnates cannot be assimilated by
the human psyche. For Poe, her story could never be written;
it could only be rewritten, over and over, obsessively, like the
repetition of some hideous drama of revivification.

Fear as a Theme in Poe's Work

Michael L. Burduck

Michael L. Burduck is a professor of American literature at Tennessee Technological University in Cookeville. In the following article, Burduck contends that Poe used fear to intrigue his readers—to probe what author Stephen King calls "phobic pressure points." By having his fictional characters encounter fear and conquer it, Poe is providing his readers with a cathartic experience.

Fear plays a key role in Poe's tales. Most of the characters in the Gothic pieces find themselves slaves of this emotion. Skilled craftsman and artist as he is, Poe realizes that he must also lure his readers into a web of fear. His use of fear, then, must be directed at both artistically created figures and the readers who will either leave the book or remain spellbound by the story and follow it eagerly toward its conclusion. Poe relies on what Stephen King in *Danse Macabre* (1981) calls "phobic pressure points." Common to all members of a particular society, such points make them react to the horrors presented in a tale or novel. The good horror writer will exploit these inner fears as he strives to terrorize his readers. Attempting to reach as large an audience as possible, Poe decided to use the fears present in the nineteenth-century mind as the means of luring his readers into his fictive world.

How well did Poe succeed in grasping his readers with the embrace of fear? Perhaps the words of his contemporary Philip Pendleton Cooke demonstrate the effectiveness of his fear-ridden narratives. In a letter dated 4 August 1846 Cooke describes his reaction to one of Poe's tales, and he leaves little doubt as to its effect: . . .

> I have always found some one remarkable thing in your stories to haunt me long after reading them. The *teeth* in

Excerpted from *Grim Phantasms: Fear in Poe's Short Fiction* by Michael L. Burduck (New York: Garland, 1992). Copyright ©1992 by Michael L. Burduck. Reprinted by permission of the author.

> Berenice—the changing eyes of Morella—the red & glaring
> crack in the House of Usher . . . the visible drops falling into
> the goblet in Ligeia, & c. & c.—there is always something of
> this sort to stick by the mind.

Although two years later Cooke would suggest that Poe's appeal might increase if he wrote about subjects nearer ordinary life, his thoughts attest the power of fear present in Poe. No doubt other readers shared Cooke's views and found themselves terrified in broad daylight as they read a Poe tale.

The psychological machinations of human beings fascinated Poe: "he was always eager to arrive at exact analyses of qualities of mind." Attempting to chart the hidden mazes of thought became for him a lifelong artistic quest. Of all the emotions produced by and affecting the mind, fear most intrigued Poe. Influenced by Edmund Burke, Poe knew that no other passion so effectively prevents the mind from acting or reasoning. Like his narrator in "Usher," Poe sought to discover the true sources and nature of fear. Throughout his fiction he probed the mind in order better to understand this grim phantasm, which at one time or another holds every man in its grasp. . . .

THE DEPTHS OF PSYCHIC DARKNESS

Readers often categorize Poe's fear sketches as morbid. His concentration on such matters as bizarre death and torture leads some to doubt his sanity. Others consider Poe a literary pioneer. Commenting on Poe's stories, Norman Foerster recognizes Poe's use "of ugly and harrowing things from which men automatically avert their eyes, of the strange functioning of the senses, the nerves, the subconscious self." Foerster views the bizarre characteristics of Poe's stories as an artist's attempt to treat all of man's emotions. H.P. Lovecraft also praises Poe and his horror fiction:

> He saw clearly that all phases of life and thought are equally
> eligible as subject matter for the artist . . . and decided to be
> the interpreter of those powerful feelings and frequent happenings which attend pain rather than pleasure, decay rather
> than growth, terror rather than tranquility.

Realizing the power of pain, decay, and terror, Poe explored these feelings and attempted to enlighten the dark tunnels of human life. Like some of his contemporaries, Poe challenged the rather overly optimistic ideas formulated at the onset of the American Renaissance. Whereas certain of his literary colleagues would have shrunk back, Poe forged his way toward a better understanding of life and all of its aspects. He attempted to bring his literary light into the depths of psychic darkness [as critic Lowry Nelson argues]: "the monstrous seems to have led more significantly to a fictional discovery of the true depths of human nature than to a mere exploitation of the sensational and the perverse." The depths of fear were not the least of Poe's concerns. . . .

Through his acquaintance with such works as Benjamin Rush's *Medical Inquiries and Observations upon the Diseases of the Mind,* published in 1812, Poe familiarized himself with the fears recorded by the pioneers of modern American psychology. Such early psychological treatises helped to shape Poe's perspectives regarding fear and madness. He learned what scared the nineteenth-century reader, and he consciously strummed those inner chords buried deep in his readers' minds.

SOME CHARACTERISTICS OF THE GOTHIC

Before examining Poe's strategy of fear, we should study briefly some of the pervasive qualities in Gothic tales. Scholars have spilled a great deal of critical ink discussing the tale of terror. Since Poe decided to use this genre as his chief means of relaying his artistic vision, a few comments concerning this form of fiction may help to clarify the relationship between Poe and the tradition with which he worked.

Originating with the publication in 1864 of Horace Walpole's *The Castle of Otranto,* Gothic fiction became a popular type of literature. Sinister castles, cruel villains, helpless victims clanking chains, and supernatural visitors entranced the reading public. Writers of these tales were eager to explore new horizons in their works. Eighteenth-century literature had previously placed great emphasis on the mind's rational power. Order and reason reigned supreme. Many writers, consequently, produced works that adhered to a carefully planned Neoclassical formula. *The Castle of Otranto* helped to produce a counterforce against rigid Neoclassicism. Rejecting art that called attention to its own artifice, poets created works arising from the depths of the imagination. This new form of Romantic literature stressed the importance of emotion. Instead of imitating established conventions, writers would now admit the powers of emotion and seek to instill their works with an original imaginative quality shunned by more conservative literary figures.

Apart from allowing authors to examine new literary territory, how did the Gothic strike its intended audience? To many readers the term "Gothic" conveyed the idea of barbarism. Some of the stock devices of Gothic fiction no doubt contributed to such a view. Despite the surface horrors evident in virtually all such tales, Gothicism appealed to some spiritual wellspring buried deep within each member of its audience. Critics realized that such fiction satisfied [according to critic Edith Birkhead] "the human desire to experience new emotions and sensations without actual danger.". . . Gothic fiction provides its audience with the sorts of adventures that help them to forget the dull trivialities of everyday life. The mundane falls victim to the fantastic. Gothic stories permit the members of the public to visit exotic lands and to meet mysterious people such as they would otherwise never encounter. The Gothic in this respect becomes a type of escape reading, a form of entertainment which permits the reader's imagination to carry him into the author's fictive world. . . .

Gothic writers use tangible horrors to subdue the reader's emotions and draw him farther into the dark abyss of fear: [according to critic Philip P. Hallie] "Horror is an experience of cruelty being exerted fascinatingly and violently by a single personal force upon a single personal victim.". . . Poe uses fear as the force that assails the victim's body and mind. Burke feels that physical and mental violence are closely related:

> The only difference between pain and terror, is, that things which cause pain operate on the mind, by the intervention of the body; whereas things that cause terror generally affect the bodily organs by the operation of the mind suggesting the danger.

The interaction of mind and body plays an important part in the reader's perception of fear, and Burke's remarks about terror help to demonstrate how the Gothic concerns itself with psychological and, often, sexual reality.

Two terms mentioned by Burke and Hallie have received considerable critical attention. "Terror" and "horror," despite their similarities, possess slightly different connotations when used in the study of Gothic fiction. In the opinion of [critic Devendra P.] Varma, the power of terror resides in the uncertainty and obscurity that I accompany it. Not knowing what lurks behind the locked door terrifies the reader. Being unable to ascertain the source of anxiety places one in the realm of terror. Terror gives way to horror when the reader finally confronts whatever being or event lies at the heart of his fears: "the difference between terror and horror is the difference between the awful apprehension and sickening realization: between the smell of death and stumbling against a corpse.". . . .

The Gothic story relying on the internal machinations of the mind captures exploiting psychological fears. Resisting vampires or demons proves difficult, but certain protective measures do exist. Unfortunately no wreath of garlic or pentagram can protect the mind from itself. Although he uses some of the externally oriented trappings of the terror-Gothic, Poe directs himself more toward the horrors of the human mind. He prefers to scare his audience from within. . . .

In light of all the points discussed thus far the Gothic becomes an imaginative exercise rooted in psychological reality. Fictitious characters fall victim to the realistic human emotion of fear. By presenting such episodes the Gothic writer produces an anodyne which assists the reader in confronting life's stresses. Although fear persists and remains firmly embedded in the human psyche, the reader who faces it in fiction might also refuse to succumb when he encounters it in his own life. The thoughts of Varma support such an opinion when he states "the Gothic novelists touched the concealed, glorious, *intrinsically healthy* [Burduck's italics] primeval power that lay restlessly palpitating under the sophistication and form of the Augustan Age." Terror and horror used properly in the Gothic might actually benefit the reading public. A reader could explore his own mental caverns as he perused a Gothic tale and learn something about himself. As an examination of his use of Gothic tradition reveals, Poe cleverly relies on his knowledge of the Gothic's true power.

POPULAR TASTE AND THE HUMAN MIND

Poe acknowledges the power of fear and realizes that the Gothic tale provides a useful means of discussing this emotion. His use of Gothicism revolves strategically around his efforts to produce an extremely popular form of literature to attract readers. The tales must spellbind and capture the audience's complete attention. Popular taste becomes very important for Poe. In his fiction he strives to appeal to his contemporaries through the use of fear. Recognizing fear's alluring qualities, he entices the reader into entering not only the world of the particular tale but also the depths of his own consciousness.

Reviews concerning Poe's fiction reveal that despite an occasional unfavorable notice many critics found his work appealing. Unable to achieve financial success, Poe managed to reach a good number of readers, thanks to the popular annuals, newspapers, and magazines. His contributions to these publications permitted him to evolve a variety of symbolist terror that has never been surpassed. The public read these tales of terror and provided Poe with an opportunity to use his fear formula. Besides contributing fiction and poetry to various literary journals, Poe served as editor for a number of prominent nineteenth-century magazines. With the help of his friend John Pendleton Kennedy he became assistant editor for T.W. White's *Southern Literary Messenger.* Later he worked for other periodicals including *Burton's Gentleman's Magazine, Graham's Magazine,* and *The Broadway Journal.*

Magazines appealed to an audience possessing a wide range of literary interests. Articles appearing in these journals discussed such topics as domestic and foreign politics, religion, farming, sociology, and science. For the more literarily inclined members of the populace, the editors included fiction, poetry, essays, and literary criticism. Some of the popular periodicals of the 1830s, including the renowned *Blackwood's Magazine,* regularly featured tales using two motifs which intrigued the typical nineteenth-century reader: the adventure to exotic places and the death of a beautiful young lady. These themes figure significantly in much of Poe's fiction, and we can see the influence that popular fiction of the period played in the development of his stories.

Familiarity with the trends evident in magazine literature gave Poe valuable information regarding reading taste. He learned what sort of literature was popular and what type of fiction the public wanted. Concerned with maintaining a high literary tradition no less than with profit, he would excite his reader's imagination with an art geared toward the audience's psychological response to it. No better type of literature to achieve this end existed than that which explored the nature and effects of fear.

Poe makes an interesting remark in his "Marginalia" in the June 1849 issue of the *Southern Literary Messenger*: "the nose of a mob is its imagination. By this, at any time, it can be quietly led." Disliking the notion of a poorly educated "mob," Poe realizes that all people, even those not intelligent enough to appreciate the finer points of art, react when their imaginations are stimulated. A work that tempts the imagination automatically appeals to readers. Arousing readers' curiosity helps the writer to insure the popularity of his fiction. Through his work with the magazines of his day Poe possessed a firm knowledge of both popular taste and the functioning of the human mind. Armed with such information he spearheaded an attack deep into the psychological realm of fear.

THE APPEAL OF FEAR

In all his Gothic fiction, Poe remains aware of the curious appeal of fear, terror, and horror. For some reason these elements attract readers. As Lovecraft remarks, "Poe so clearly and realistically understood the natural basis of the horror-appeal . . . ." Knowing how readers readily devoured fiction featuring murder, torture, disease, and death, Poe incorporated these features into his tales. Various critics speculate on the reasons behind the attraction to fear. Edmund Burke provides a philosophical basis regarding fear and a person's desire to experience it. Poe seems to be aware of Burke's theories concerning this matter and uses these ideas as he creates his tales.

Commenting on the origins of the term "fear," Burke shows that the Latin *stupeo* means fear or astonishment. On the basis of this revelation Poe and other readers could see the similarity between fear and wonder. A person may become terrified in a particular situation but still express wonder as he contemplates his predicament. Beauty exists side by side with terror and horror. Various spectacles in the natural world and, one must assume, mental perceptions as well, produce such experience. Burke speculates:

> Whatever is fitted in any sort to excite the ideas of pain and danger, that is to say, whatever is in any sort terrible, or is conversant about terrible objects or operates in a manner analogous to terror, is a source of the *sublime;* that is, it is productive of the strongest emotion which the mind is capable of feeling.

For Burke, then, the sublime elevates one's mind to the point where a person becomes attracted to the source of such stimulation. Some of the qualities that produce the sublime include obscurity, power, privation, vastness, infinity, difficulty, magnificence, and loudness. . . .

Burke believes that pain and danger possess the ability to delight the mind. He uses the example of physical exercise to illustrate his point. The pain resulting from such action provides delight because it relieves the boredom of inactivity. Such pain also helps one develop a strong body. Along with physical activity, mental liveliness also benefits a person. The active, well-developed mind keeps one alert and permits one to face whatever mental challenges arise. One of the most intense problems the mind encounters is that presented by pain and fear. Both recognizing and facing this condition delight a person because he must exercise his mental faculties to conquer his misgivings.

Poe accepts Burke's theories regarding the production of the sublime. Faced with terror, the mind must grapple with the paradoxical responses of dread and desire. Burke, however, fails to describe such events as "pleasurable" because pain does not directly produce pleasure. Is there some legitimate way for terror to please a reader? [Critic Terry] Heller suggests that Poe relies on terror's ability to fill the reader with a feeling of satisfaction:

> The pleasure of reading a tale which to some degree attempts a direct attack of terror on the reader derives from the reader's successful exercise of his faculties of personal integration in resistance to the threats posed by the story.

This concept presupposes that the writer can draw his reader from his own society into the "world" of the tale. Becoming a part of the author's fictive universe, the reader gratifies himself by enduring those fears that overcome the protagonists. By personalizing the story, the author makes his audience imaginatively experience the fear present in the work. Poe understands this process and attempts to capture his reader with it.

FACING FEAR

Like most other Gothic writers, Poe knows that terror and horror are social and relational rather than original or private. All humans struggle against the same basic fears. Such battles prove necessary because they help us to confront life's unpleasant realities. Running from fear might even produce unhealthy consequences. Poe feels that "the attempt to escape may only intensify . . . horror." One brief example from Poe's fiction illustrates this point. In "Usher," Roderick manages to bring about his own madness and death by refusing to face and conquer fear. The tale traces the history of his gradual descent into the realm of terror and madness. He becomes a passive victim of "the grim phantasm." Perhaps his situation would have been different if he had earlier faced his fears bravely. Instead he waited helplessly for fear and superstition to annihilate him.

Poe advises his readers not to retreat in the face of fear. Although enduring stress often proves painful, Poe, along with D.H. Lawrence, knows that "the human soul must suffer its own disintegration, consciously, if ever it is to survive." Encountering boldly the demons lurking in the dungeons of the mind becomes the first step in exorcising these troublesome creatures. No doubt Poe desired to show his readers the necessity of navigating the tempests of life. Fear can produce knowledge and courage if one exhibits a certain amount of tenacity.

The strategy of fear devised by Poe depends upon his knowledge of nineteenth-century readers and their popular tastes. Familiar with the operation of the mind, Poe relies on the horror-appeal present in human thought. Fear intrigues as it frightens us. Aware of the terror tale's popularity, Poe uses fear as the bait to attract readers into his Gothic world. To obtain the best possible results, Poe deliberately takes advantage of the particular fears present in the typical nineteenth-century mind. Knowledge of these "phobic pressure points" allows Poe to produce tales directed toward a reader's psychic weaknesses. He understands what specific fears exist in his contemporaries and accordingly exploits them.

Poe's Use of Allegory

Richard Wilbur

Richard Wilbur is best known as a poet and was nominated America's poet laureate in 1987. He has taught English at Harvard and Wesleyan University. While a member of the Society of Fellows at Harvard he began to study Poe. In the following article, taken from a lecture delivered at the Library of Congress in 1959, Wilbur analyzes both Poe's poetry and his tales, illuminating the allegorical touches within them. Wilbur believes that Poe's tales remain "the best things of their kind in our literature."

Like many romantic poets, Poe identified imagination with dream. Where Poe differed from other romantic poets was in the literalness and absoluteness of the identification, and in the clinical precision with which he observed the phenomena of dream, carefully distinguishing the various states through which the mind passes on its way to sleep. A large number of Poe's stories derive their very structure from this sequence of mental states: *Ms. Found in a Bottle,* to give but one example, is an allegory of the mind's voyage from the waking world into the world of dreams, with each main step of the narrative symbolizing the passage of the mind from one state to another—from wakefulness to reverie, from reverie to the hypnagogic state, from the hypnagogic state to the deep dream. The departure of the narrator's ship from Batavia represents the mind's withdrawal from the waking world; the drowning of the captain and all but one of the crew represents the growing solitude of reverie; when the narrator is transferred by collision from a real ship to a phantom ship, we are to understand that he has passed from reverie, a state in which reality and dream exist in a kind of equilibrium, into the free fantasy of the hypnagogic state. And when the phantom ship makes its final plunge into the whirlpool, we are to understand that the narrator's mind has

Excerpted from "The House of Poe," the 1959 Library of Congress Anniversary Lecture, by Richard Wilbur, as reprinted in *The Recognition of Edgar Allan Poe*, edited by Eric W. Carlson (Ann Arbor: University of Michigan Press, 1966). Reprinted by permission of the author.

gone over the brink of sleep and descended into dreams.

What I am saying by means of this example is that the scenes and situations of Poe's tales are always concrete representations of states of mind. If we bear in mind Poe's fundamental plot—the effort of the poetic soul to escape all consciousness of the world in dream—we soon recognize the significance of certain scenic or situational motifs which turn up in story after story. The most important of these recurrent motifs is that of *enclosure* or *circumscription*; perhaps the latter term is preferable, because it is Poe's own word, and because Poe's enclosures are so often more or less circular in form. The heroes of Poe's tales and poems are violently circumscribed by whirlpools, or peacefully circumscribed by cloud-capped Paradisal valleys; they float upon circular pools ringed in by steep flowering hillsides; they dwell on islands, or voyage to them; we find Poe heroes also in coffins, in the cabs of balloons, or hidden away in the holds of ships; and above all we find them sitting alone in the claustral and richly furnished rooms of remote and mouldering mansions.

Almost never, if you think about it, is one of Poe's heroes to be seen standing in the light of common day; almost never does the Poe hero breathe the air that others breathe; he requires some kind of envelope in order to be what he is; he is always either enclosed or on his way to an enclosure. The narrative of William Wilson conducts the hero from Stoke Newington to Eton, from Eton to Oxford, and then to Rome by way of Paris, Vienna, Berlin, Moscow, Naples, and Egypt: and yet, for all his travels, Wilson seems never to set foot out-of-doors. The story takes place in a series of rooms, the last one locked from the inside.

Sometimes Poe emphasizes the circumscription of his heroes by multiple enclosures. Roderick Usher dwells in a great and crumbling mansion from which, as Poe tells us, he has not ventured forth in many years. This mansion stands islanded in a stagnant lake, which serves it as a defensive moat. And beyond the moat lies the Usher estate, a vast barren tract having its own peculiar and forbidding weather and atmosphere. You might say that Roderick Usher is defended in depth; and yet at the close of the story Poe compounds Roderick's inaccessibility by having the mansion and its occupant swallowed up by the waters of the tarn.

What does it mean that Poe's heroes are invariably enclosed or circumscribed? The answer is simple: circumscription, in Poe's tales, means the exclusion from consciousness of the so-called real world, the world of time and reason and physical fact; it means the isolation of the poetic soul in visionary reverie or trance. When we find one of Poe's characters in a remote valley, or a claustral room, we know that he is in the process of dreaming his way out of the world. . . .

THE MEANING OF DECAY

I have said that Poe saw the poet as at war with the material world, and with the material or physical aspects of himself; and I have said that Poe identified poetic imagination with the power to escape from the material and the materialistic, to exclude them from consciousness and so subjectively destroy them. Now, if we recall these things, and recall also that the exteriors of Poe's houses or palaces, with their eye-like windows and mouth-like doors, represent the physical features of Poe's dreaming heroes, then the characteristic dilapidation of Poe's architecture takes on sudden significance. The extreme decay of the House of Usher—a decay so extreme as to approach the atmospheric—is quite simply a sign that the narrator, in reaching that state of mind which he calls Roderick Usher, has very nearly dreamt himself free of his physical body, and of the material world with which that body connects him.

This is what decay or decomposition mean everywhere in Poe; and we find them almost everywhere. Poe's preoccupation with decay is not, as some critics have thought, an indication of necrophilia; decay in Poe is a symbol of visionary remoteness from the physical, a sign that the state of mind represented is one of almost pure spirituality. When the House of Usher disintegrates or dematerializes at the close of the story, it does so because Roderick Usher has become all soul. *The Fall of the House of Usher,* then, is not really a horror story; it is a triumphant report by the narrator that it is possible for the poetic soul to shake off this temporal, rational, physical world and escape, if only for a moment, to a realm of unfettered vision. . . .

Poe's typical building . . . is set apart in a valley or a sea or a waste place, and this remoteness is intended to express the retreat of the poet's mind from worldly consciousness into dream. It is a tottery structure, and this indicates that the dreamer within is in that unstable threshold condition called the hypnagogic state. Finally, Poe's typical building is crumbling or decomposing, and this means that the dreamer's mind is moving toward a perfect freedom from his material self and the material world. Let us now open the door—or mouth—of Poe's building and visit the mind inside. . . .

THE SHAPE OF POE'S ROOMS

The first thing to notice about Poe's dream-rooms is their shape. It has already been said that the enclosures of Poe's tales incline to a curving or circular form. And Poe himself, in certain of his essays and dialogues, explains this inclination by denouncing what he calls "the harsh mathematical reason of the schools," and complaining that practical science has covered the face of the earth with "rectangular obscenities." Poe quite explicitly identifies regular angular forms with everyday reason, and the circle, oval, or fluid arabesque with the otherworldly imagination. Therefore, if we discover that the dream-chambers of Poe's fiction are free of angular regularity, we may be sure that we are noticing a pointed and purposeful consistency in his architecture and décor.

The ball-room of the story *Hop-Frog* is circular. The Devil's apartment in *The Duc de l'Omelette* has its corners "rounded into niches," and we find rounded corners also in Poe's essay *The Philosophy of Furniture*. In *Ligeia*, the bridal chamber is a pentagonal turret-room; however, the angles are concealed by sarcophagi, so that the effect is circular. The corners of Roderick Usher's chamber are likewise concealed, being lost in deep shadow. Other dream-rooms are either irregular or indeterminate in form. For example, there are the seven rooms of Prince Prospero's imperial suite in *The Masque of the Red Death*. As Poe observes, "in many palaces . . . such suites form a long and straight vista"; but in Prince Prospero's palace, as he describes it, "the apartments were so irregularly disposed that the vision embraced but little more than one at a time. There was a sharp turn at every twenty or thirty yards, and at each turn a novel effect." The turret-room of *The Oval Portrait* is not defined as to shape; we are told, however, that it is architecturally "bizarre," and complicated by a quantity of unexpected nooks and niches. Similarly, the visionary's apartment in *The Assignation* is described only as dazzling, astounding and original in its architecture; we are not told in what way its dimensions are peculiar, but it seems safe to assume that it would be a difficult room to measure for wall-to-wall carpeting. The room of *The Assignation,* by the way—like that of *Ligeia*—has its walls enshrouded in rich figured draperies which are continually agitated by some mysterious agency. The fluid shifting of the figures suggests, of course, the behavior of hypnagogic images; but the agitation of the draperies would also produce a perpetual ambiguity of architectural form, and the effect would resemble that which Pevsner ascribes to the interior of San Vitale in Ravenna: "a sensation of uncertainty [and] of a dreamlike floating."

Poe, as you see, is at great pains to avoid depicting the usual squarish sort of room in which we spend much of our waking lives. His chambers of dream either approximate the circle—an infinite form which is, as Poe somewhere observes, "the emblem of Eternity"—or they so lack any apprehensible regularity of shape as to suggest the changeableness and spatial freedom of the dreaming mind. The exceptions to this rule are few and entirely explainable. I will grant, for instance, that the iron-walled torture-chamber of *The Pit and the Pendulum* portrays the very reverse of spatial freedom, and that it is painfully angular in character, the angles growing more acute as the torture intensifies. But there is very good allegorical reason for these things. The rooms of *Ligeia* or *The Assignation* symbolize a triumphantly imaginative state of mind in which the dreamer is all but free of the so-called "real" world. In *The Pit and the Pendulum,* the dream is of quite another kind; it is a nightmare state, in which the dreamer is imaginatively impotent, and can find no refuge from reality, even in dream. Though he lies on the brink of the pit, on the very verge of the plunge into unconsciousness, he is still unable to disengage himself from the physical and temporal world. The physical oppresses him in the shape of lurid graveyard visions; the temporal oppresses him in the form of an enormous and deadly pendulum. It is altogether appropriate, then, that this particular chamber should be constricting and cruelly angular. . . .

LIGHTING

We have spoken of the winding approaches to Poe's dream-chambers, of their curvilinear or indeterminate shape, and of the rich eclecticism of their furnishings. Let us now glance over such matters as lighting, sound-proofing, and ventilation. As regards lighting, the rooms of Poe's tales are never exposed to the naked rays of the sun, because the sun belongs to the waking world and waking consciousness. The narrator of *The Murders in the Rue Morgue* tells how he and his friend Dupin conducted their lives in such a way as to avoid all exposure to sunlight. "At the first dawn of the morning," he writes, "we closed all the messy shutters of our old building; lighting a couple of tapers which, strongly perfumed, threw out only the ghastliest and feeblest of rays. By the aid of these we then busied our souls in dreams...."

In some of Poe's rooms, there simply are no windows. In other cases, the windows are blocked up or shuttered. When the windows are not blocked or shuttered, their panes are tinted with a crimson or leaden hue, so as to transform the light of day into a lurid or ghastly glow. This kind of lighting, in which the sun's rays are admitted but transformed, belongs to the portrayal of those half-states of mind in which dream and reality are blended. Filtered through tinted panes, the sunlight enters certain of Poe's rooms as it might enter the half-closed eyes of a day-dreamer, or the dream-dimmed eyes of someone awakening from sleep. But when Poe wishes to represent that deeper phase of dreaming in which visionary consciousness has all but annihilated any sense of the external world, the lighting is always artificial and the time is always night.

Flickering candles, wavering torches, and censors full of writhing varicolored flames furnish much of the illumination of Poe's rooms, and one can see the appropriateness of such lighting to the vague and shifting perceptions of the hypnagogic state. But undoubtedly the most important lighting-fixture in Poe's rooms—and one which appears in a good half of them—is the chandelier. It hangs from the lofty ceiling by a long chain, generally of gold, and it consists sometimes of a censer, sometimes of a lamp, sometimes of candles, sometimes of a glowing jewel (a ruby or a diamond), and once, in the macabre tale *King Pest,* of a skull containing ignited charcoal. What we must understand about this chandelier, as Poe explains in his poem *Al Aaraaf,* is that its chain does not stop at the ceiling: it goes right on through the ceiling, through the roof, and up to heaven. What comes down the chain from heaven is the divine power of imagination, and it is imagination's purifying fire which flashes or flickers from the chandelier. That is why the immaterial and angelic Ligeia makes her reappearance directly beneath the chandelier; and that is why Hop-Frog makes his departure for dream-land by climbing the chandelier-chain and vanishing through the sky-light.

The dreaming soul, then, has its own light—a light more spiritual, more divine, than that of the sun. And Poe's chamber of dream is autonomous in every other respect. No breath of air enters it from the outside world: either its atmosphere is dead, or its draperies are stirred by magical and intramural air currents. No earthly sound invades the chamber: either it is deadly still, or it echoes with a sourceless and unearthly music. Nor does any odor of flower or field intrude: instead, as Poe tells in *The Assignation,* the sense of smell is "oppressed by mingled and conflicting perfumes, reeking up from strange convolute censers.". . .

ALLEGORICAL FIGURES

The typical Poe story occurs *within* the mind of a poet; and its characters are not independent personalities, but allegorical figures representing the warring principles of the poet's divided nature. The lady Ligeia, for example, stands for that heavenly beauty which the poet's soul desires; while Rowena stands for that earthly, physical beauty which tempts the poet's passions. The action of the story is the dreaming soul's gradual emancipation from earthly attachments—which is allegorically expressed in the slow dissolution of Rowena. The result of this process is the soul's final, momentary vision of the heavenly Ligeia. Poe's typical story presents some such struggle between the visionary and the mundane; and the duration of Poe's typical story is the duration of a dream.

There are two tales in which Poe makes an especially clear and simple use of his architectural symbolism. The first is an unfamiliar tale called *The System of Dr. Tarr and Prof. Fether,* and the edifice of that tale is a remote and dilapidated madhouse in southern France. What happens, in brief, is that the inmates of the madhouse escape from their cells in the basement of the building, overpower their keepers, and lock them up in their own cells. Having done this, the lunatics take possession of the upper reaches of the house. They shutter all the windows, put on odd costumes, and proceed to hold an uproarious and discordant feast, during which there is much eating and drinking of a disgusting kind, and a degraded version of Ligeia or Helen does a strip-tease. At the height of these festivities, the keepers escape from their cells, break in through the barred and shuttered windows of the dining-room, and restore order.

Well: the madhouse, like all of Poe's houses, is a mind. The keepers are the rational part of that mind, and the in-mates are its irrational part. As you noticed, the irrational is suitably assigned to the cellar. The uprising of the inmates, and the suppression of the keepers, symbolizes the begin-ning of a dream, and the mad banquet which follows is per-haps Poe's least spiritual portrayal of the dream-state: *this* dream, far from being an escape from the physical, consists exclusively of the release of animal appetites—as dreams sometimes do. When the keepers break in the windows, and subdue the revellers, they bring with them reason and the light of day, and the wild dream is over.

The Masque of the Red Death is a better-known and even more obvious example of architectural allegory. You will re-call how Prince Prospero, when his dominions are being ravaged by the plague, withdraws with a thousand of his knights and ladies into a secluded, impregnable and win-dowless abbey, where after a time he entertains his friends with a costume ball. The weird decor of the seven ballrooms expresses the Prince's own taste, and in strange costumes of the Prince's own design the company dances far into the night, looking, as Poe says, like "a multitude of dreams." The festivities are interrupted only by the hourly striking of a gi-gantic ebony clock which stands in the westernmost room; and the striking of this clock has invariably a sobering effect on the revellers. Upon the last stroke of twelve, as you will remember, there appears amid the throng a figure attired in the blood-dabbled grave-clothes of a plague-victim. The dancers shrink from him in terror. But the Prince, infuriated at what he takes to be an insolent practical joke, draws his dagger and pursues the figure through all of the seven rooms. In the last and westernmost room, the figure sud-denly turns and confronts Prince Prospero, who gives a cry of despair and falls upon his own dagger. The Prince's friends rush forward to seize the intruder, who stands now within the shadow of the ebony clock; but they find nothing there. And then, one after the other, the thousand revellers fall dead of the Red Death, and the lights flicker out, and

Prince Prospero's ball is at an end.

In spite of its cast of one thousand and two, *The Masque of the Red Death* has only one character. Prince Prospero is one half of that character, the visionary half; the nameless figure in grave-clothes is the other, as we shall see in a moment.

A DISEASED AGE

More than once, in his dialogues or critical writings, Poe describes the earth-bound, time-bound rationalism of his age as a *disease.* And that is what the Red Death signifies. Prince Prospero's fight from the Red Death is the poetic imagination's fight from temporal and worldly consciousness into dream. The thousand dancers of Prince Prospero's costume ball are just what Poe says they are—"dreams" or "phantasms," veiled and vivid creatures of Prince Prospero's rapt imagination. Whenever there is a feast, or carnival, or costume ball in Poe, we may be sure that a dream is in progress.

But what is the gigantic ebony clock? For the answer to that, one need only consult a dictionary of slang: we call the human heart a *ticker,* meaning that it is the clock of the body; and that is what Poe means here. In sleep, our minds may roam beyond the temporal world, but our hearts tick on, binding us to time and mortality. Whenever the ebony clock strikes, the dancers of Prince Prospero's dream grow momentarily pale and still, in half-awareness that they and their revel must have an end; it is as if a sleeper should half-awaken, and know that he has been dreaming, and then sink back into dreams again.

The figure in blood-dabbled grave-clothes, who stalks through the terrified company and vanishes in the shadow of the clock, is waking, temporal consciousness, and his coming means the death of dreams. He breaks up Prince Prospero's ball as the keepers in *Dr. Tarr and Prof. Fether* break up the revels of the lunatics. The final confrontation between Prince Prospero and the shrouded figure is like the terrible final meeting between William Wilson and his double. Recognizing his adversary as his own worldly and mortal self, Prince Prospero gives a cry of despair which is also Poe's cry of despair: despair at the realization that only by self-destruction could the poet fully free his soul from the trammels of this world.

Poe's aesthetic, Poe's theory of the nature of art, seems to me insane. To say that art should repudiate everything

human and earthly, and find its subject-matter at the flickering end of dreams, is hopelessly to narrow the scope and
function of art. Poe's aesthetic points toward such impover-
ishments as *poésie pure* and the abstract expressionist movement in painting. And yet, despite his aesthetic, Poe is a great
artist, and I would rest my case for him on his prose alle-
gories of psychic conflict. In them, Poe broke wholly new
ground, and they remain the best things of their kind in our
literature. Poe's mind may have been a strange one; yet all
minds are alike in their general structure; therefore we can
understand him, and I think that he will have something to
say to us as long as there is civil war in the palaces of men's
minds.

Humor in Poe's Tales

James H. Justus

James H. Justus was professor of English at Indiana University and has written on a wide variety of American authors, including Nathaniel Hawthorne, Ernest Hemingway, William Faulkner, and Robert Penn Warren. In the following excerpt, Justus points out that while Poe is often viewed as morbid and excessively ornate in his writing, many readers fail to understand that Poe is being humorous. Justus goes on to give examples of Poe's humor.

Poe's comic sense can be both curiously old-fashioned and presciently fashionable. If he sometimes resembles a collegiate humorist in naming an editor 'Scissors' or in playing rhyming games with a law firm ('Bogs, Hogs, Logs, Frogs & Co.') and a gentleman's ancestry on the distaff side (Froissart-Croissart-Voissart-Moissart), at other times Poe sounds like a trendy philosopher; he likes the peculiarly jocular manner of storytelling in one novel he reviews 'inasmuch as to say "I know I am writing nonsense, but then you must excuse me for the very reason that I know it."' In that same novel, *Sheppard Lee*, Poe delights in its author's *bizarreries* by which nine of the hero's siblings die within six years 'by a variety of odd accidents—the last expiring in a fit of laughter at seeing his brother ridden to death by a pig'.

In the preface to his first collection of fiction, *Tales of the Grotesque and Arabesque* (1840), Poe would seem to invite us into a region not exclusively Gothic. By this time he had already gained the reputation he would continue to have for the next century: as the author of 'the wild—unnatural and horrible!'—the result of a fatal 'German enchantment'. Poe acknowledges the Germanic flavour of some of his tales, but then remarks curiously: 'Tomorrow I may be anything but German, as yesterday I was everything else'—a playful statement that semantically seems to deny *any* German taint or,

Excerpted from "Poe's Comic Vision and Southwestern Humour" by James Justus, in *Edgar Allan Poe: The Design of Order*, edited by A. Robert Lee (Totowa, NJ: Barnes and Noble Books, 1987). Copyright ©1987 by Vision Press Ltd. Reprinted by permission of Barnes and Noble Books.

alternately, that congenially projects himself into whatever categories his critics prepare for him. Poe's first book of fiction contains twenty-five tales, at least eleven of which are wholly comic in intent. The forms and moods range widely. While the satiric burlesques of popular genres most decisively reveal Poe as the wide-awake and competitive magazinist, one suspects that the broader, more farcical tales reflect a truer side of the man, the Poe who extracts grim humour out of physical discomfiture, violence, and death.

The two drunk sailors of 'King Pest' are caricatures more than characters: Legs is six-and-a-half feet tall, stooped, thin, hawk-nosed, chinless; Hugh Tarpaulin is four feet tall, bowlegged, small-eyed, thick-lipped, purple-faced. With the gestures of stage comedians they dominate their literally dead environment, plague-ridden London streets, and their kinetic highjinks propel them down some stairs and into the circumscribed space that Poe usually reserves for his Gothic tales: a wine cellar, abandoned except for six victims in the latter stages of disease. Against the simple drunken appetitiveness of the sailors Poe juxtaposes the pettiness and vanity of a mock-court playing at illusory life. The grim carousel, amid skeletons and still unburied corpses, of a gaunt company soon to be both erupts in slapstick rebellion and violence. For all its repulsive subject matter, 'King Pest' is marked by its creator's usual fondness for puns, literary allusions, and mock-allegorical names. As T.O. Mabbott shows, Poe liked it well enough to revise meticulously.

'FOUR BEASTS IN ONE'

Poe's artistry in the revising of his comic tales generally is more striking than his originality. For all the individualizing effects that go to make these tales indisputably Poesque, their origins—in continental literature, English romanticism, American writing, and contemporary newspapers—range from the classical to the ephemera of popular journalism. Two of his most good-natured thrusts at human pride are free adaptations of ancient narrative forms. An early sketch, 'Four Beasts in One', is a variation on the fairy tale about the emperor's new clothes; and a later story, 'The Spectacles', is based on the old joke about the man who discovers that his beautiful wife is an old hag artfully disguised. The latter situation allows Poe to use the practical joke as moral corrective: a young man who out of pride refuses to wear needed eyeglasses is easily tricked into courting and marrying his great-great-grandmother. For the king who dresses in the hide of a beast 'for the better sustaining his dignity as king', the reversal of the hierarchical status of man and beast is willed in madness: 'With how superior a dignity the monarch perambulates on all fours!' His subjects dutifully hail him Prince of Poets and Glory of the East, but when in a sudden mutiny the kingly fortunes change, human instinct reasserts itself and the Prince of Poets is 'upon his hinder legs, running for his life'. This droll exercise reveals a Poe fully participating in such mainstream literary themes as the vagaries of power and fame, the beast within the man, and the thin line separating the flattering public and the raging mob.

The human urge of a perverse king or a foolish young man to reshape reality to suit a more idealized vision always comes to grief in Poe's humorous pieces. In some ways that lesson, repeated in various narrative combinations, paradoxically underscores a darker vision of the nature of man than his outright tales of terror, clotted as they are with such esoterica as metempsychosis and diabolism. In his serious assaults on the mysteries, Poe's fascination with one of the ultimate questions—What is Man?—is obsessive, but his answers, approached from diverse perspectives, remain exploratory, tentative. In the comic pieces Poe's mind is settled. They may dramatize his view of man-as-beast, a bundle of biological attributes that the ego foolishly elevates to something higher; or, just as often, they depict man-as-mechanism—a collection of cogs, pumps, conduits. In either instance, the famous yearning for supernal ideality that we so often associate with Poe is conspicuously missing.

It is doubtless true that Poe's comedy is primarily satiric, trimmed here and there with turns from vaudeville and the theatre of farce. Important to this formulation, of course, is a not-so-hidden indignation at the spectacle of life itself. Scholar [Stephen L. Mooney] asserts that the function of Poe's brand of satire is 'the exposure of a society in which heroes and rulers are shown to be deluded or irresponsible and their subjects a dehumanized, sycophantic mass'. Such specificity explains the cautionary 'Four Beasts in One', the grim gallows humour of 'Hop-Frog', and that more genial exercise in turned tables, 'The System of Doctor Tarr and Professor Fether'. And although explaining a writer's sense of humour is only a little easier than explaining a joke, it would seem that in addition to the social motive of exposure, Poe's forays into comedy are often self-revelations of the most personal kind.

'A TALE OF JERUSALEM'

The pseudo-biblical prose of 'A Tale of Jerusalem', for example, is an over-elaborate dressing for a simple ethnic joke, a faintly scatological tale of discomfiture in which the besieging Romans respond to the Jewish request for a sacrificial Sabbath lamb by substituting 'a *hog* of no common size'. There is no reason to think that Poe in his maturity did not continue to think this extended joke funny; like other lesser efforts he carefully revised this one. Another kind of self-revelation shows up in 'thou Art the Man', a ratiocinative tale in which a good-humoured, neighbourly old gentleman turns out to be the murderer. The brutal handling of the victim's corpse for the purpose of extracting a confession narratively and morally justifies the dénouement, but it does not explain the gusto with which the detective-narrator thrusts a stiff whalebone down the throat of his friend, now a 'bruised, bloody and nearly putrid corpse', transforming it into a jack-in-the-box that will pop up at an expeditious moment.

What is both publicly exposed and privately revealed is human fallibility in a vision of man that seems darker in its comic versions than in its serious, partly because of a technique of cheerfully indiscriminate pastiche. Though Poe may begin with conventional satiric purposefulness, he dilutes it with exaggeration, caricature, puns and other wordplay, farce, literary burlesque, even private jokes. The comic sense in Poe often emerges from the very proliferation of such devices, and though they may be funny in themselves, they crowd and nudge each other to the point where satiric intent is smudged. In the serious tales, we may quarrel over the meaning of 'Ligeia' or 'The Fall of the House of Usher', but we tend to accept the author's boast that nothing in them is extraneous, no detail that does not contribute to the unity of his chosen effect. But only someone who is haunted by separation and disjunction could make so much of the principle of unity. The harmony of parts coalescing into the whole is finally more important than what the whole means. The famous tales of death are themselves dead—intensely coherent constructions featuring marionettes posturing against painted backdrops. In his theoretical essays his tortured metaphors—the steady pressure of the stamp upon the wax, the dropping of the water on the rock—celebrate the mechanical process by which Poe thinks proper literature gets written.

POE'S HUMOROUS TALES ARE LESS CONTRIVED

In certain respects we get a more transparent, less mediated Poe in his comedy, where the psychic aggression is more open, because there is no pretended harmony of their units. [Poe scholar Thomas] Mabbott once remarked that Poe believed 'all wholly inappropriate combinations comic'. Indeed, the mismatched parts and crude rivets help to shape the jerry-built structures into symbolic artifacts of Poe's vision, and their message reads: there is no harmony in man or society. The sheer juxtaposition of pratfalls, mock-Gothicism, wit, parody, buffoonery, and personal pique points to a reality ununified and an actuality of disproportion. In an early sketch, 'The Assignation', the stranger-hero shapes his environment to accord with his insight into the absurdity of life; the interior of his palazzo, a riotous hodge-podge of incongruous styles and embellishments, is almost a pre-parodic version of those harmonious and extravagant interiors so lovingly detailed in the mature fiction. 'Some things are so completely ludicrous that a man *must* laugh or die', says the Byronic protagonist. He does both.

In his relentless exploration of man, Poe finds convenient the available and conventional scientific assumptions about the human body; when he literalizes them, they invariably dramatize the deflation of man, and the process of human reductiveness becomes comic. The Brevet Brigadier General of 'The Man that was Used Up', formerly a famous Indian fighter, is introduced as the most imposing personage in Philadelphia society. Poe first telegraphs the real ordinariness of his hero by naming him John A.B.C. Smith before he finally reduces him to a nondescript bundle over which the narrator nearly stumbles. The hero with an *air distingué* turns out to be a human fragment with assorted mechanical devices to fill him out: artificial leg, arms, shoulders, bosom, wig, teeth, eye—all capped with an ingenious palate, a contrivance that turns the general's natural squeaks into sonorous booms. The narrator of 'Loss of Breath' searches in his *boudoir* for his lost breath, finding instead 'a set of false teeth, two pairs of hips, an eye, and a bundle of *billets-doux* from Mr. Windenough to [his] wife'. Although this story begins as a verbal joke—the literalization of a common expression—it develops, like the modern cartoon, through a series of debilitating physical encounters. In Mr. Lackobreath's declension, a surgeon cuts off his ears, two cats fight over his nose, he suffers a fractured skull and broken arms, and, mistaken on a stagecoach for an object of convenience, he is finally used as a makeshift mattress. The corporeal stripping away is also a psychological reduction, and the curiously deadpan tone of the first-person narrator intensifies this masochistic fantasy.

Allen Tate once recalled the pride of his ancestors in being able to claim Poe as one of their own because 'nothing that Mr. Poe wrote, it was said soon after his death, could bring a blush to the cheek of the purest maiden.' Perhaps mid-nineteenth-century maidens were more doughty than their late nineteenth-century legend, or perhaps they were merely selective. The kind of tastelessness that made Victorians blush—corporeal explicitness—is usefully forestalled in Poe's lyrics by obfuscation and esoteric allusion, but in the fiction the potential offence of the bad taste is pre-empted by surprise, the *frisson* of revelation: bloody cerements, infused gore of corpses, simian indelicacy with a woman's body. If the visceral emphasis in Poe's fiction did not cause maidens to blush, did it ever make them sick? Gross visceral actuality even informs some of those pieces based on Poe's fascination with scientific discoveries of his day.

'THE CASE OF M. VALDEMAR'

In 'The Case of M. Valdemar', the serious experiment of extending life to the dying by mesmeric trance is undercut by a grim relish in its inevitable and messy failure. By tinkering, Valdemar's bodily degeneration is slowed until nature asserts itself over the artificial and speeds up the processes. It is an experiment conducted without regard for the victim's distraught pleas: 'quick!—quick!—put me to sleep—or, quick!—waken me!—quick!—*I say to you that I am dead!*' Valdemar is denied the dignity of his own death: 'his whole frame', reports the narrator, 'crumbled—absolutely *rotted* away beneath my hands. Upon the bed, before that whole company, there lay a nearly liquid mass of loathsome—of detestable putridity.' The final detail, towards which this otherwise indifferent tale moves, is of course meant to be shocking. But the horror of visceral transformation—a tootoo solid flesh reduced in the twinkling of an eye to disgusting jelly—is also linked, I think, to what Henry James and T.S. Eliot saw generally as Poe's arrested development at the pre-adolescent stage. The Valdemar denouement is a displaced child's joke, suggesting that period when the young, after years of private absorption and training in their own bodily mechanisms, socialize the fascination, converting the most natural functions into the most elemental humour. Ingestion, digestion, evacuation—with all that the nose smells and the ear hears—become public phenomena to be appreciated as comedic spectacles. This linkage of gross corporeality and childish humour does not comport well with the image of Poe the metaphysical yearner, but it grimly supports the underlying seriousness of Poe's dark view of the human species; to be mindful of man is to be mindful of how a seemingly stable solid is really a fragile envelope of gases and liquids into which the entire organism finally dissolves.

'SOME WORDS WITH A MUMMY'

More explicitly, the feat in 'Some Words with a Mummy', bringing Count Allamistakeo back to life, disintegrates into childish oral competition between the scientists and the now-voluble mummy. The satire in this tale is directed against nineteenth-century progress as represented by the voltaic pile and the galvanic battery, but Poe's vaudeville imagination constantly threatens to submerge the satire. Dandifying the mummy into an acerb snob in order to dismiss progress is a recognizable variation on Poe's eighteenth-century models in which visitors from exotic lands visit and evaluate modern civilization, but allowing the mummy to give a swift kick to his resuscitator's groin is slapstick business borrowed from the farcical theatre and the practical jokes of the frontier humorists. . . .

POE'S HUMOROUS PARADOXES

Even in his own day Poe's humour asked readers to imagine more deeply than they were normally willing to do. To perceive the nature of man and society through Poesque spectacles was to see sanity in madness, the lifeless in the breathing, the corpse in the living body, the joker in the ordered universe—and to think of these paradoxes as funny.

For a writer who described himself as 'not of the merry mood', Poe produced a remarkable amount of 'unserious' fiction. As Mabbott's edition of the prose fiction shows, in terms of sheer bulk nearly half is overtly comic; and G.R. Thompson has argued persuasively that even the gothic fiction that we normally read as straight contains more than trace elements of the comic. In the last decade scholars have unearthed a writer of such monumental duplicity that the dominant image of Poe the exploiter of terror and sensation may eventually be replaced by that of the witty self-parodist and burlesque comedian. How 'merry' his comic prose may be is another question, of course. Certainly the social reality in 'Doctor Tarr and Professor Fether' and 'Loss of Breath' is as imaginatively skewed as that in 'Berenice' and 'The Black Cat'—the laugher they generate is laced with mockery.

Poe's Use of Horror

Edward H. Davidson

Edward H. Davidson was a professor of English at
the University of Illinois. In the following article,
excerpted from his book *Poe: A Critical Study*,
Davidson analyses Poe's use of horror and all of its
effects. Davidson believes that by using horror, Poe
was able to inquire "into special states of mind.
[Horror] was a means to externalize, in vivid physical objects, inner states of being and a method of
portraying the mind's awareness of itself."

Death and horror would seem to be associated, and indeed
they must be in any investigation of the mind and art of Poe.
But we must consider the theme of horror as something
apart and as available for inquiry for its own sake. We must
also consider this theme . . . as contained in both the poetry
and the short stories, though our emphasis will of necessity
fall on the poetry. Yet it was such a theme as that of death or
horror which binds Poe's story-writing career to his poetic
experience and writing; by only slightly shifting the emphasis and the rhetorical devices he could write "tales of horror" just as ably as he had written poems of horror, and then
come back, in his later life, to write poems of death and horror again. One might easily draw a line from the very early
"Tamerlane" through "The Fall of the House of Usher" to
"The Raven": all of them were studies of stages in consciousness when the real world slipped away or disinte-
grated and the mind found itself fronting the "horror" of its
own loneliness and loss.

First of all, we might define the Poesque version of horror
as that region or mysterious middle ground where the normal, rational faculties of thinking and choice have, for reasons beyond knowing, been suspended; ethical and religious
beliefs are still the portion of men, but are powerless to function. All power of choice and all sense of direction have been

Reprinted by permission of the publisher from *Poe: A Critical Study* by Edward H.
Davidson (Cambridge, MA: Harvard University Press). Copyright ©1957 by the President and Fellows of Harvard College.

lost; in fact, they have been so long lost that the nightmare world of presumed reality obeys no laws of reason or stability. It is a highly complex metaphysical condition wherein the constants of heaven and hell are fixed at their opposite polarity, but between them is the vast region wherein the human will is situated and is powerless to effect any variation of its own existence. It is a realm where the will cannot exist, not because it never had an existence but because it somehow lost its power to function. It is a world like that in "The City in the Sea": moral man once lived in that long-ago world, but now everything is shadowy and atrophied. In such a horror world men are moral mutes or paralytics; they are like Roderick Usher, the "Last of the Visigoths," at the very end of a long line of ethically directed ancestors. Horror is, then, the urgent need for moral knowledge and direction—and its total lack. The characters in such a situation can only dream of a condition which once existed but which they would never be able to follow, even if they were able to recapture it. They are like the creatures in Poe's most complete allegorical presentations, those in the apocalyptic visions like "The Conversation of Eiros and Charmion" (1839) and "The Colloquy of Monos and Una" (1841): they are the victims of an Apocalypse which has had no perceptible reason for being. . . .

With Poe we are hardly concerned with "evil". . . insofar as evil might be considered inherent in man or in the phenomenal order; in a sense, his one prescription for evil is its absence: never to know evil nor to have been engaged in any moral struggle is the condition of horror in which the Poe protagonist must exist. In such a nightmare world all the prescriptions for evil and good are matters for nostalgia and regret; they were part of some other state of being from which man has moved or which has long passed from the earth. Only when these protagonists are, like Michaelangelo in "Al Aaraaf" or the strange creatures in "Silence" or "The Colloquy of Monos and Una," on, as it were, the "other side" can they at last realize what it was they never knew. . . .

HORROR AS PSYCHOLOGY

Horror was . . . not only a philosophy or a method of explaining the mystery of the universe; it was also "psychology" or a method of inquiring into special states of mind. It was a means to externalize, in vivid physical objects, inner states of being and a method of portraying the mind's awareness of itself. These "objects" of horror were not themselves necessarily horrible; they were what they were because a mind saw them and was even destroyed by them. In one way this was Poe's contribution to the dark subliminal literature of a later time: he demonstrated that states of consciousness are not simply isolated conditions of madness but are somehow intimately and intricately related to the physical world around it. Poe's fault (to hasten ahead of our exposition for a moment) was that, once he had found a vivid externalization for a condition of inner consciousness—a crack in the wall, a black cat, a portrait, an insistent heartbeat—the physical exemplification assumed command; and in the succeeding narrative, whether in poem or in short story, the objectification was out of all proportion to the inner condition. One might say that the symbol ran away with the idea; Poe was content to let the convulsive dance of objectified forms enact the drama. Thus rhetoric and landscape conveyed the agony.

Taken altogether, these conditions of consciousness which Poe exposed did not suggest that Poe was revealing himself or aspects of his own inner being but was actually detailing certain stages and varieties of what might be termed the "Romantic consciousness." Horror was therefore Poe's insight into Romantic self-consciousness—into the tendency of the Romantic mind to consider that its own psychic response to life and to the world was a sufficient subject for life. The tendency need not have ended in "horror"; it did end in the capacity of the Romantic mind both to create and to be almost simultaneously scrutinizing itself at the moment of creative activity. . . .

WASTED ANGUISH

What marks Poe's studies of a man caught in some inner or outer horror is that, for all the sufferings the protagonist must undergo, the fictive "I" never learns anything. The anguish is wasted because the sufferer comes out of the action precisely the same as he went into it. Nothing has really occurred "inside"; there was no inner consciousness to begin with, and the pilgrimage of the questing self had been wrought entirely in terms of the scene, the natural objects in easy accord and attendance, and the incantatory spell-weaving which somehow reduced the tangible world to a mere logarithm. The symbolic projection took precedence and triumphed over what it was originally designed to pre-figure and represent. Therefore, nothing could happen to the mind caught in the terror of an event; everything must happen to the outside world which is made to envision the agony. All the while the mind remains unmoved. . . .

Poe's world of the mind was limited to the world of primary sensation and to the terrors which afflict children. It was the boy's erotic world without any sense or knowledge of Eros: women become the victims of horror; they are married, they suffer (only Morella ever bore a child, and it was a monster), they die or are killed; and they were all the while the sacrificial victims to a mere man, not the Romantic hero-god.

We might account for this externalization of inner states of being not only on the score that Poe's mind did not deeply search the infinitely variable symbolisms between itself and exterior reality by which reality itself is transformed as Melville transformed the universe from the crow's nest, but also on the supposition of the rhetorical or language problem. Poe was enormously successful in his own day, as he still is in ours, because he somehow arranged a set of well-known counters that would inevitably give his readers the shudders. But he did so at his own cost.

While in his poetry he was dedicated to giving new meanings to the poetic imagination, in his prose tales Poe was content to employ a set of invariable metaphors which would be, for him, immediately clear. Thus the names for exterior objects became an instantaneous direction for the mind to follow between the idea and its externalization. Every state of mind had, therefore, a readily known representation. The language of prose (we must be careful to insist that this was not Poe's theory of the language of poetry) consisted of a set of metaphors by which anything could be presented: a lion is a strong man, a fox a cunning man, a grave the terror and anguish of death, the underground cavern the secret past, a plague the terror of the invisible world, and so on. Throughout Poe's tale-writing career these metaphors remained almost invariable; they had no power of yielding to the unique circumstance. Perhaps to his own age these devices were vivid because they had not been too long in the literary domain; in a later time they command little interest not so much because they may be worn out as because they bring only a moment's connotation. . . .

THE RITUAL OF DEATH

One of the curiosities of Poe's treatment of death was that death became a very elaborate ritual: just as the New England Puritan from Samuel Sewall to Emily Dickinson wanted to know every step of the way by which a friend or relative had left this world and gone to the next, so Poe was the laureate in the manner of proper, gentlemanly dying. But one element marks all these deaths, however horrifying they may be: they are all apocalypses; that is, they all concern the time before and the time after death; they do not portray that moment of anguish and loss of being which has formed so much of the imaginative experience in American literature from Edward Taylor to Hemingway. With Poe, the fact of death is very much like the Crucifixion narrative which ends with the Cross and resumes when the stone is found rolled away from the tomb. The god or man did not really die; he merely shifted his location. One stage stops at the final glimpse of death; the other begins already on the other side, and, imaginatively, we have never really gone through.

Such a view and treatment lend themselves very readily to the apocalyptic method. That is, the death of one person is magnified into a universal catastrophe, just as at the death of Christ the graves opened, the veil of the temple was rent, and the sky darkened. [Two] of these apocalyptic visions are Poe's striving to present the ultimate symbolism of death.

The [earlier of the two] is "Silence, A Fable" (1838). The tale begins where "Al Aaraaf" left off, that is, with Ezekiel's Old Testament view of last things. The "waters of the river" do not flow to the sea but have "a tumultuous and convulsive motion"; for miles on either side of the river are vast regions of "gigantic water-lilies." Beyond as far as the horizon is a "horrible" and endless forest. Situated somewhere in his vast desert of whiteness and convulsed waters is "a huge gray rock" upon which the moon shines and reveals the mystic word "Desolation." The protagonist of the narrative has a demon's power to call up spirits from dead bodies. He summons the hippopotami who come to the foot of "Desolation" rock and roar "loudly and fearfully beneath the moon." Then, at the end, the protagonist curses the silence; all the elements obey: the sun stands still; the thunder dies away; the lightning dims, and all matter reverts to its primal condition of utter and endless deadness. At the last the crepuscular light shines on the mystic rock and reveals the word "Silence."

The tale is hardly more than a sketch and crudely approximates the vision-literature such as in Ezekiel ("And the lynx which dwelleth forever in the tomb, came out therefrom, and lay down at the feet of the Demon, and looked at him steadily in the face."). It is a curious mixture of the spell-binding Protestant evangelism of the 1830's with the sensationalist rhetoric in the magazines. What the tale does, however, is to make the universe engage in the catastrophe; it is a projection of a kind of "cosmic unconscious" which drives the assumed order of nature back to its primordial condition. What Poe is fumbling to express is the idea he worked out with such care in *Eureka*: the history of the universe is an expression of a law; and that law states that all matter had a single locus, a primal Oneness, from which it was dispersed throughout all space. In time the dispersive force will be withdrawn, and all matter will return to its primal unity, its Ur-condition again. What Poe was trying to express by the mystic word "Desolation" was the presently observed state of total disunity and by the term "Silence" the inevitable coalescence of all substance.

"The Conversation of Eiros and Charmion" (1839), titled on its appearance in 1843 "The Destruction of the World," is a continuation of this apocalyptic vision of what might happen to the physical and intellectual universe when it exists beyond horror, that is, when discontinuity and incoherence are constants rather than aberrations. As the story opens we are situated beyond life and death; indeed, we have passed through and have reached the state from which we can view death from the comfortable vantage of hindsight. Then we retrace our way and consider the steps leading to the death of the world: a passing comet extracted all the nitrogen from the atmosphere surrounding the earth and left the highly flammable air ready for a spark to set off a terrible cosmic explosion. In the debacle, however, only the earth was destroyed; thus there came about "the entire fulfillment, in all their minute and terrible details, of the fiery and horror-inspiring denunciations of the prophecies of the Holy Book."

What Poe has here attempted to do is to establish a historical and symbolic relationship between myth, or prophecy, and the scientifically known constitution of the universe: the assumption is that what physics and chemistry have latterly revealed, Jewish scripture and Oriental legend have long anticipated. There is, consequently, a demonstration of the universal law of both matter and being which functions from Unity to dispersal and back to Unity again; this principle is so basic to the whole universe that not only the physical constitution but the very elements of thought itself are symbolic exemplifications of its eternal operation. . . .

HORROR AS MORALITY

These tales were Poe's rationalizations of horror; that is, the principle of horror itself seems to imply that the horrific is that which suddenly interrupts or shatters the rational order of the universe; however completely that order is restored, the human mind forced to endure that "apocalypse" or shock will be forever dislocated or maddened. The young man in "The Raven" will never recover his "soul" or his acceptance of the coherence of things after his terrible insight, not only into his own madness, but into the madness of the universe itself. The young man in "The Pit and the Pendulum" was able to maintain his sanity by the power of his will to escape the swinging knife-blade just long enough to be fortuitously rescued from a private psychic world which every moment threatened him with insanity and annihilation. These and other inquiries into the dark world of the mind suggest that Poe, however much his horror was a rather simple externalization of inner states of being, was demonstrating that horror itself or various phases of loss of self might be ways into farther and deeper understanding. Horror, madness, and death are man's avenues into the ultimate rationale of existence of which our own mortal existence is but a crude fragment. Man in his earthly habit lives on the virtually unquestioned assumption that he can predict and understand nearly every event that occurs in his own life and in the diurnal motions of the planets; Poe, however much his rhetoric may have been apocalyptic and frenzied and his narrative struggling to be *outré*, was nevertheless writing a series of quite moral poems and tales concerning the evidence everywhere before man's eyes of the total disunity and incoherence of his own life which is an infinitesimal part of the universal "plot of God." Man must, however, be terrified or driven to comprehend that what seems to be fractured is actually a segment of the universal design and what appears to be madness may be "divinest sense."

Occasionally Poe treated this theme in such a tale as "The

Fall of the House of Usher," a masterpiece of horror . . . , or in his further studies of the crack-up of a human mind. In *Eureka*, published in the next to the last year of his life, Poe made a final and thorough investigation of the principles of unity to diffusion and back to unity again, principles which underlay the theory and practice of the horror poem and tale in his earlier years.

CHAPTER 3

A Critical Selection

Poe Explains "The Raven"

Edgar Allan Poe

Though critics have doubted such deliberate calculation is possible, Poe claims to have had the ability to analyze his intentions and mental steps as he worked. One of Poe's commentaries, "The Philosophy of Composition," presented here, records Poe's explanation of how he wrote and interpreted his most well known poem, "The Raven."

I have often thought how interesting a magazine paper might be written by any author who would—that is to say, who could—detail, step by step, the processes by which any one of his compositions attained its ultimate point of completion. Why such a paper has never been given to the world, I am much at a loss to say—but, perhaps, the authorial vanity has had more to do with the omission than any one other cause. Most writers—poets in especial—prefer having it understood that they compose by a species of fine frenzy—an ecstatic intuition—and would positively shudder at letting the public take a peep behind the scenes, at the elaborate and vacillating crudities of thought—at the true purposes seized only at the last moment—at the innumerable glimpses of idea that arrived not at the maturity of full view—at the fully matured fancies discarded in despair as unmanageable—at the cautious selections and rejections—at the painful erasures and interpolations—in a word, at the wheels and pinions—the tackle for scene-shifting—the step-ladders and demon-traps—the cock's feathers, the red paint and the black patches, which, in ninety-nine cases out of the hundred, constitute the properties of the literary *histrio* [actor].

I am aware, on the other hand, that the case is by no means common, in which an author is at all in condition to retrace the steps by which his conclusions have been at-

Edgar Allan Poe, "The Philosophy of Composition," in *The Writer's Art: By Those Who Have Practiced It*, edited by Rollo Walter Brown (Cambridge, MA: Harvard University Press, 1921).

tained. In general, suggestions, having arisen pell-mell, are pursued and forgotten in a similar manner.

For my own part, I have neither sympathy with the repugnance alluded to, nor, at any time, the least difficulty in recalling to mind the progressive steps of any of my compositions; and, since the interest of an analysis, or reconstruction, such as I have considered a *desideratum* [something desired], is quite independent of any real or fancied interest in the thing analyzed, it will not be regarded as a breach of decorum on my part to show the *modus operandi* by which some one of my own works was put together. I select "The Raven," as the most generally known. It is my design to render it manifest that no one point in its composition is referrible either to accident or intuition—that the work proceeded, step by step, to its completion with the precision and rigid consequence of a mathematical problem.

Let us dismiss, as irrelevant to the poem *per se*, the circumstance—or say the necessity—which, in the first place, gave rise to the intention of composing a poem that should suit at once the popular and the critical taste.

We commence, then, with this intention.

ON LENGTH

The initial consideration was that of extent. If any literary work is too long to be read at one sitting, we must be content to dispense with the immensely important effect derivable from unity of impression—for, if two sittings be required, the affairs of the world interfere, and every thing like totality is at once destroyed. But since, *ceteris paribus,* no poet can afford to dispense with *any thing* that may advance his design, it but remains to be seen whether there is, in extent, any advantage to counterbalance the loss of unity which attends it. Here I say no, at once. What we term a long poem is, in fact, merely a succession of brief ones—that is to say, of brief poetical effects. It is needless to demonstrate that a poem is such, only inasmuch as it intensely excites, by elevating, the soul; and all intense excitements are, through a psychal necessity, brief. For this reason, at least one half of the "Paradise Lost" is essentially prose—a succession of poetical excitements interspersed, *inevitably,* with corresponding depressions—the whole being deprived, through the extremeness of its length, of the vastly important artistic element, totality, or unity, of effect.

It appears evident, then, that there is a distinct limit, as regards length, to all works of literary art—the limit of a single sitting—and that, although in certain classes of prose composition, such as "Robinson Crusoe," (demanding no unity,) this limit may be advantageously overpassed, it can never properly be overpassed in a poem. Within this limit, the extent of a poem may be made to bear mathematical relation to its merit—in other words, to the excitement or elevation again in other words, to the degree of the true poetical effect which it is capable of inducing; for it is clear that the brevity must be in direct ratio of the intensity of the intended effect:—this, with one proviso—that a certain degree of duration is absolutely requisite for the production of any effect at all.

Holding in view these considerations, as well as that degree of excitement which I deemed not above the popular, while not below the critical, taste, I reached at once what I conceived the proper *length* for my intended poem—a length of about one hundred lines. It is, in fact, a hundred and eight.

BEAUTY

My next thought concerned the choice of an impression, or effect, to be conveyed: and here I may as well observe that, throughout the construction, I kept steadily in view the design of rendering the work *universally* appreciable. I should be carried too far out of my immediate topic were I to demonstrate a point upon which I have repeatedly insisted, and which, with the poetical, stands not in the slightest need of demonstration—the point, I mean, that Beauty is the sole legitimate province of the poem. A few words, however, in elucidation of my real meaning, which some of my friends have evinced a disposition to misrepresent. That pleasure which is at once the most intense, the most elevating, and the most pure, is, I believe, found in the contemplation of the beautiful. When, indeed, men speak of Beauty, they mean, precisely, not a quality, as is supposed, but an effect—they refer, in short, just to that intense and pure elevation of *soul—not* of intellect, or of heart—upon which I have commented, and which is experienced in consequence of contemplating "the beautiful." Now I designate Beauty as the province of the poem, merely because it is an obvious rule of Art that effects should be made to spring from direct causes—that objects should be attained through means best adapted for their attainment—no one as yet having been weak enough to deny that the peculiar elevation alluded to, is *most readily* attained in the poem. Now the object, Truth, or the satisfaction of the intellect, and the object Passion, or the excitement of the heart, are, although attainable, to a certain extent, in poetry, far more readily attainable in prose. Truth, in fact, demands a precision, and Passion, a *homeliness* (the truly passionate will comprehend me) which are absolutely antagonistic to that Beauty which, I maintain, is the excitement, or pleasurable elevation, of the soul. It by no means follows from any thing here said, that passion, or even truth, may not be introduced, and even profitably introduced, into a poem—for they may serve in elucidation, or aid the general effect, as do discords in music, by contrast—but the true artist will always contrive, first, to tone them into proper subservience to the predominant aim, and, secondly, to enveil them, as far as possible, in that Beauty which is the atmosphere and the essence of the poem.

Regarding, then, Beauty as my province, my next question referred to the *tone* of its highest manifestation—and all experience has shown that this tone is one of *sadness.* Beauty of whatever kind, in its supreme development, invariably excites the sensitive soul to tears. Melancholy is thus the most legitimate of all the poetical tones.

THE REFRAIN

The length, the province, and the tone, being thus determined, I betook myself to ordinary induction, with the view of obtaining some artistic piquancy which might serve me as a key-note in the construction of the poem—some pivot upon which the whole structure might turn. In carefully thinking over all the usual artistic effects—or more properly *points,* in the theatrical sense—I did not fail to perceive immediately that no one had been so universally employed as that of the *refrain.* The universality of its employment sufficed to assure me of its intrinsic value, and spared me the necessity of submitting it to analysis. I considered it, however, with regard to its susceptibility of improvement, and soon saw it to be in a primitive condition. As commonly used, the *refrain,* or burden, not only is limited to lyric verse, but depends for its impression upon the force of monotone—both in sound and thought. The pleasure is deduced solely from the sense of identity—of repetition. I resolved to diversify, and so vastly heighten, the effect, by adhering, in general, to the monotone of sound, while I continually varied that of thought: that is to say, I determined to produce continuously novel effects, by the variation *of the application* of the *refrain*—the *refrain* itself remaining, for the most part, unvaried.

These points being settled, I next bethought me of the *nature* of my *refrain*. Since its application was to be repeatedly varied, it was clear that the *refrain* itself must be brief, for there would have been an insurmountable difficulty in frequent variations of application in any sentence of length. In proportion to the brevity of the sentence, would, of course, be the facility of the variation. This led me at once to a single word as the best *refrain*.

The question now arose as to the *character* of the word. Having made up my mind to a *refrain*, the division of the poem into stanzas was, of course, a corollary: the *refrain* forming the close to each stanza. That such a close, to have force, must be sonorous and susceptible of protracted emphasis, admitted no doubt: and these considerations inevitably led me to the long *o* as the most sonorous vowel, in connection with *r* as the most producible consonant.

The sound of the *refrain* being thus determined, it became necessary to select a word embodying this sound, and at the same time in the fullest possible keeping with that melancholy which I had predetermined as the tone of the poem. In such a search it would have been absolutely impossible to overlook the word "Nevermore." In fact, it was the very first which presented itself.

CONCEPT

The next *desideratum* was a pretext for the continuous use of the one word "nevermore." In observing the difficulty which I at once found in inventing a sufficiently plausible reason for its continuous repetition, I did not fail to perceive that this difficulty arose solely from the pre-assumption that the word was to be so continuously or monotonously spoken by *a human* being—I did not fail to perceive, in short, that the difficulty lay in the reconciliation of this monotony with the exercise of reason on the part of the creature repeating the word. Here, then, immediately arose the idea of a *non*-reasoning creature capable of speech; *and*, very naturally, a parrot, in the first instance, suggested itself, but was superseded forthwith by a Raven, as equally capable of speech, and infinitely more in keeping with the intended *tone*.

I had now gone so far as the conception of a Raven—the bird of ill omen—monotonously repeating the one word, "Nevermore," at the conclusion of each stanza, in a poem of melancholy tone, and in length about one hundred lines. Now, never losing sight of the object *supremeness,* or perfection, at all points, I asked myself—"Of all melancholy topics, what, according to the *universal* understanding of mankind, is the *most* melancholy?" Death—was the obvious reply. "And when," I said, "is this most melancholy of topics most poetical?" From what I have already explained at some length, the answer, here also, is obvious—"When it most closely allies itself to *Beauty*: the death, then, of a beautiful woman is, unquestionably, the most poetical topic in the world—and equally is it beyond doubt that the lips best suited for such topic are those of a bereaved lover."

A Dialogue

I had now to combine the two ideas, of a lover lamenting his deceased mistress and a Raven continuously repeating the word "Nevermore"—I had to combine these, bearing in mind my design of varying, at every turn, the *application* of the word repeated; but the only intelligible mode of such combination is that of imagining the Raven employing the word in answer to the queries of the lover. And here it was that I saw at once the opportunity afforded for the effect on which I had been depending—that is to say, the effect of the *variation of application.* I saw that I could make the first query propounded by the lover—the first query to which the Raven should reply "Nevermore"—that I could make this first query a commonplace one—the second less so—the third still less, and so on—until at length the lover, startled from his original *nonchalance* by the melancholy character of the word itself—by its frequent repetition—and by a consideration of the ominous reputation of the fowl that uttered it—is at length excited to superstition, and wildly propounds queries of a far different character—queries whose solution he has passionately at heart—propounds them half in superstition and half in that species of despair which delights in self-torture—propounds them not altogether because he believes in the prophetic or demoniac character of the bird (which, reason assures him, is merely repeating a lesson learned by rote) but because he experiences a phrenzied pleasure in so modeling his questions as to receive from the *expected* "Nevermore" the most delicious because the most intolerable of sorrow. Perceiving the opportunity thus afforded me—or, more strictly, thus forced upon me in the progress of the construction—I first established in mind the climax, or concluding query—that to which "Nevermore" should be in the last place an answer—that in reply to which this word "Nevermore" should involve the utmost conceivable amount of sorrow and despair.

Here then the poem may be said to have its beginning—at the end, where all works of art should begin—for it was here, at this point of my preconsiderations, that I first put pen to paper in the composition of the stanza:

> "Prophet," said I, "thing of evil! prophet still if bird or devil!
> By that heaven that bends above us—by that God we both
>   adore,
> Tell this soul with sorrow laden, if within the distant Aidenn,
> It shall clasp a sainted maiden whom the angels name
>   Lenore—
> Clasp a rare and radiant maiden whom the angels name
>   Lenore."
>   Quoth the raven "Nevermore."

I composed this stanza, at this point, first that, by establishing the climax, I might the better vary and graduate, as regards seriousness and importance, the preceding queries of the lover—and, secondly, that I might definitely settle the rhythm, the metre, and the length and general arrangement of the stanza—as well as graduate the stanzas which were to precede, so that none of them might surpass this in rhythmical effect. Had I been able, in the subsequent composition, to construct more vigorous stanzas, I should, without scruple, have purposely enfeebled them, so as not to interfere with the climacteric effect.

ORIGINALITY

And here I may as well say a few words of the versification. My first object (as usual) was originality. The extent to which this has been neglected, in versification, is one of the most unaccountable things in the world. Admitting that there is little possibility of variety in mere *rhythm*, it is still clear that the possible varieties of metre and stanza are absolutely infinite—and yet, *for centuries, no man, in verse, has ever done, or ever seemed to think of doing, an original thing.* The fact is, originality (unless in minds of very unusual force) is by no means a matter, as some suppose, of impulse or intuition. In general, to be found, it must be elaborately sought, and although a positive merit of the highest class, demands in its attainment less of invention than negation.

Of course, I pretend to no originality in either the rhythm or metre of the "Raven." The former is trochaic—the latter is octameter acatalectic, alternating with heptameter catalectic repeated in the *refrain* of the fifth verse, and terminating with tetrameter catalectic. Less pedantically—the feet employed throughout (trochees) consist of a long syllable followed by a short: the first line of the stanza consists of eight of these feet—the second of seven and a half (in effect two-thirds)—the third of eight—the fourth of seven and a half—the fifth the same—the sixth three and a half. Now, each of these lines, taken individually, has been employed before, and what originality the "Raven" has, is in their *combination into stanza*; nothing even remotely approaching this combination has ever been attempted. The effect of this originality of combination is aided by other unusual, and some altogether novel effects, arising from an extension of the application of the principles of rhyme and alliteration.

SETTING

The next point to be considered was the mode of bringing together the lover and the Raven—and the first branch of this consideration was the *locale*. For this the most natural suggestion might seem to be a forest, or the fields—but it has always appeared to me that a close *circumscription of space* is absolutely necessary to the effect of insulated incident:—it has the force of a frame to a picture. It has an indisputable moral power in keeping concentrated the attention, and, of course, must not be confounded with mere unity of place.

I determined, then, to place the lover in his chamber—in a chamber rendered sacred to him by memories of her who had frequented it. The room is represented as richly furnished—this in mere pursuance of the ideas I have already explained on the subject of Beauty, as the sole true poetical thesis.

The *locale* being thus determined, I had now to introduce the bird—and the thought of introducing him through the window, was inevitable. The idea of making the lover suppose, in the first instance, that the flapping of the wings of the bird against the shutter, is a "tapping" at the door, originated in a wish to increase, by prolonging, the reader's curiosity, and in a desire to admit the incidental effect arising from the lover's throwing open the door, finding all dark, and thence adopting the half-fancy that it was the spirit of his mistress that knocked.

I made the night tempestuous, first, to account for the Raven's seeking admission, and secondly, for the effect of contrast with the (physical) serenity within the chamber.

I made the bird alight on the bust of Pallas, also for the effect of contrast between the marble and the plumage—it being understood that the bust was absolutely *suggested* by the bird—the bust of *Pallas* being chosen, first, as most in keeping with the scholarship of the lover, and, secondly, for the sonorousness of the word, Pallas, itself.

About the middle of the poem, also, I have availed myself of the force of contrast, with a view of deepening the ultimate impression. For example, an air of the fantastic—approaching as nearly to the ludicrous as was admissible—is given to the Raven's entrance. He comes in "with many a flirt and flutter."

> Not the *least obseisance made he*—not a moment stopped or
>   stayed he,
> *But with mien of lord or lady,* perched above my chamber
>   door.

In the two stanzas which follow, the design is more obviously carried out:—

> Then this ebony bird beguiling my sad fancy into smiling
> By the *grave and stern decorum of the countenance it wore,*
> "Though thy *crest be shorn and shaven* thou," I said, "art
>   sure no craven,
> Ghastly grim and ancient Raven wandering from the nightly
>   shore—
> Tell me what thy lordly name is on the Night's Plutonian
>   shore!"
>   Quoth the Raven "Nevermore."

> Much I marvelled *this ungainly fowl* to hear discourse so
>   plainly,
> Though its answer little meaning—little relevancy bore;
> For we cannot help agreeing that no living human being
> *Ever yet was blessed with seeing bird above his chamber
>   door—*
> *Bird or beast upon the sculptured bust above his chamber
>   door,*
>   With such name as "Nevermore."

The Dénouement

The effect of the *dénouement* being thus provided for, I immediately drop the fantastic for a tone of the most profound seriousness:—this tone commencing in the stanza directly following the one last quoted, with the line,

> But the Raven, sitting lonely on that placid bust, spoke only,
>   etc.

From this epoch the lover no longer jests—no longer sees any thing even of the fantastic in the Raven's demeanor. He speaks of him as a "grim, ungainly, ghastly, gaunt, and ominous bird of yore," and feels the "fiery eyes" burning into his "bosom's core." This revolution of thought, or fancy, on the lover's part, is intended to induce a similar one on the part of the reader—to bring the mind into a proper frame for the *dénouement*—which is now brought about as rapidly and as *directly* as possible.

With the *dénouement* proper—with the Raven's reply, "Nevermore," to the lover's final demand if he shall meet his mistress in another world—the poem, in its obvious phase, that of a simple narrative, may be said to have its completion. So far, every thing is within the limits of the accountable—of the real. A raven, having learned by rote the single word "Nevermore," and having escaped from the custody of its owner, is driven, at midnight, through the violence of a storm, to seek admission at a window from which a light still gleams—the chamber-window of a student, occupied half in poring over a volume, half in dreaming of a beloved mistress deceased. The casement being thrown open at the fluttering of the bird's wings, the bird itself perches on the most convenient seat out of the immediate reach of the student, who, amused by the incident and the oddity of the visitor's demeanor, demands of it, in jest and without looking for a reply, its name. The raven addressed, answers with its customary word, "Nevermore"—a word which finds immediate echo in the melancholy heart of the student, who, giving utterance aloud to certain thoughts suggested by the occasion, is again startled by the fowl's repetition of "Nevermore." The student now guesses the state of the case, but is impelled, as I have before explained, by the human thirst for self-torture, and in part by superstition, to propound such queries to the bird as will bring him, the lover, the most of the luxury of sorrow, through the anticipated answer "Nevermore." With the indulgence, to the utmost extreme, of this self-torture, the narration, in what I have termed its first or obvious phase, has a natural termination, and so far there has been no overstepping of the limits of the real.

But in subjects so handled, however skilfully, or with however vivid an array of incident, there is always a certain hardness or nakedness, which repels the artistical eye. Two things are invariably required—first, some amount of complexity, or more properly, adaptation; and, secondly, some amount of suggestiveness—some under-current, however indefinite of meaning. It is this latter, in especial, which imparts to a work of art so much of that *richness* (to borrow from colloquy a forcible term) which we are too fond of confounding with *the ideal.* It is the *excess* of the suggested meaning—it is the rendering this the upper instead of the under current of the theme—which turns into prose (and that of the very flattest kind) the so called poetry of the so called transcendentalists.

Holding these opinions, I added the two concluding stanzas of the poem—their suggestiveness being thus made to pervade all the narrative which has preceded them. The under current of meaning is rendered first apparent in the lines—

"Take thy beak from out *my heart,* and take thy form from
    off my door!"
            Quoth the Raven "Nevermore!"

It will be observed that the words, "from out my heart," involve the first metaphorical expression in the poem. They, with the answer, "Nevermore," dispose the mind to seek a moral in all that has been previously narrated. The reader begins now to regard the Raven as emblematical—but it is not until the very last line of the very last stanza, that the intention of making him emblematical of *Mournful and Never-ending Remembrance* is permitted distinctly to be seen:

And the Raven, never flitting, still is sitting, still is sitting,
On the pallid bust of Pallas just above my chamber door;
And his eyes have all the seeming of a demon's that is
    dreaming,
And the lamplight o'er him streaming throws his shadow on
    the floor;
And my soul *from out that shadow* that lies floating on the
    floor
            Shall be lifted—nevermore.

"The Pit and the Pendulum": A Freudian Interpretation

Marie Bonaparte

Princess Marie Bonaparte was a disciple of the psychoanalyst Sigmund Freud. Called the father of psychoanalysis, Sigmund Freud emphasized the unconscious motives for conscious actions. He especially believed that these unconscious motives were sexual in nature. In the following article, Bonaparte reviews Poe's tale "The Pit and the Pendulum" in light of Freud's theories. Bonaparte argues that the plot of this story is an allegory about a son's fear of being annihilated by his father. Bonaparte concludes that Poe was unconsciously motivated to write many of his stories.

The Pit and the Pendulum, like our dreams or reveries, is a kind of two-part song. True, exquisitely cruel torturers might indeed construct a cell with such walls of heated metal, a yawning pit, a descending, hissing pendulum, to end their agonising victim's days. None of this is impossible and the very *plausibility* of these terrors accounts, in part, for the horror the tale inspires. But none of this explains why Poe should choose, of all possible anxiety themes, particularly these: nor above all, why these piled-up horrors should make us shudder, when many a similar invention leaves us cold.

To bring this about, these atrocities, for Poe, must have been charged with that libido which wells up from the deepest unconscious sources and communicates conviction through works of art: only thus, by ways unknown to consciousness, can the author's unconscious speak to that of his readers. And though the terror-theme of the torture cell seems superficially self-explanatory, our analytic task

Excerpted from *The Life and Works of Edgar Allan Poe: A Psycho-Analytic Interpretation* by Marie Bonaparte, translated by Joan F. Mele (London: Hogarth Press, 1949).

is to reveal the anxiety theme on which it is built, which alone gives this fearful tale its poignant and enduring impressiveness. . . .

THE INQUISITORS' TORTURE

By the villainy of the Inquisitors (who, a sort of royal "we," represent the infinitely multiplied Father), a poor wretch is doomed to a terrible punishment, certain to end in death. His crime was that he did not believe in them blindly, or submit, utterly, to their will: in short, he is guilty of heresy against the Father. But death and its approaches, here, take the form—one constant in the unconscious—of the return to the womb and that primal fœtal condition on which imagination models our future state. This wretch is immured in a deep underground cell, dark and damp though, strangely enough, he appears to have no sensation of cold. And indeed, towards the end of the tale, the then *red* walls will throw out a burning heat and, like a giant womb, begin to contract, as though to force the embryo towards the cloacal abyss. . . .

First, the doomed man miraculously escapes the pit, or premature birth, as it were. He, nevertheless, remains imprisoned, hidden and protected in the anxiety-causing womb of his grim cell. These events, and their accompanying emotions are interrupted, from time to time, by periods of semi-return to a fœtal condition; sudden lapses into deep, dreamless slumbers from which the prisoner always awakes starving but, mostly, dying of thirst. Possibly here, too, we find a memory, as in the *Narrative of Arthur Gordon Pym*, of what the little under-nourished Edgar suffered, as a result of his mother's inadequate milk?

Now, after his first escape from the cloacal birth-gulf, the prisoner wakes to find himself surrounded by sulphurous figures which cover his cell-walls: hideous demons that recall the animal totems which represent the Father in primitive minds. And when the victim lifts his eyes what, in fact, he discovers is, indeed, the castrating Father in excelsis; Time with his scythe. Yet though, in his prison, our victim is alone and desperately far from help and, though, to a certain extent, his horror of the dark corresponds to what Freud so well expresses as regards the child's fear of dark separation from the mother and loss of her protection—our victim is not, in fact, alone, for the dread eyes of invisible Fathers, from their hiding place, watch his every movement, while over and above him is the castrating Father; Time with his scythe. . . .

Here is the son garrotted, swaddled like a new-born babe, lying on his low wood cradle. Around are the walls of his cell, substituting the womb of the mother. Above, triumphant, is Father Time, with his pendulum-scythe.

And now, what does this phantasy recall? Many, in fact, often met in clinical analysis, whether of men or women. These, strange as it may seem to those unfamiliar with the phantasy-world of the unconscious, all reproduce a certain imaginary situation: that of the child imagining itself still in the womb. . . .

POE'S UNCONSCIOUS MOTIVES

In each of us, male and female are variously embodied. In men, a prime condition of health is the possession of maximum physical virility. But, in Poe, that condition seems to have been vitiated, for we know how poorly he defended that virility, and what a psychically inhibited, impotent individual he was. This, indeed, the phantasy of the tortured victim under the pendulum-scythe now, once more, indicates. . . .

Here, once again, we return to the problem of anxiety. What is the origin of the anxiety, of which this tale, as it were, is compacted? Birth anxiety, alone, cannot altogether account for it, despite the overpowering horror of the pit. Nor could separation anxiety, either, despite the victim's solitude and abandon to the dark. To me, it seems that the primordial anxiety in this tale is castration anxiety from which, more or less, stems both conscience- and death-anxiety. What menaces the victim, in the crescent of shining steel, is the slow castration-destruction of the heart. . . . And the horror of the pit, too, may well be largely fear of castration. . . .

ANXIETY IN THE TALE

As we have seen, however, this tale does not merely tell of a return to the womb in the symbol of the underground cell, its cloacal pit and contracting walls. True, part of the tale is invested with the anxiety attached to repressed incest desires—the genital danger represented by the mother, or wife, here being expressed in typical impotency fashion, *i.e.*, in terms of fœtal existence. And this face of the tale, aspected, so to speak to the mother is, at least, as anxiety-cathected—the pit being the victim's main horror—as the face aspected to the father. None the less, the father also plays an enormous part in this tale, as source of anxiety. . . .

In life, as in fiction, Poe only escaped the pit to be garrot-ted under the Pendulum. But neither there could he escape the castration threat that had made him stumble and recoil from the pit. Thus, all through life, the velleities of his ill-starred sexuality doomed him to oscillate between these dual forces, the pit and the pendulum, each luring him on but each, also, the castrator. For, to find erotic pleasure in woman he would have had to brave the pit which, however, was so constructed, following the Inquisitors' (Father, God, Creator) "most horrible plan" that there no *"sudden* extinc-tion of life" would be possible. . . .

The victim only escapes the pit to be ligatured under the pendulum, and only escapes that to be redelivered, in-escapably, to the pit, owing to the cell's womb-like contract-ing walls. Only General Lasalle; (possibly, to Poe's uncon-scious, a surrogate of the good General Lafayette, in contrast to the bad John Allan); only the good father, a *deus ex machina,* by a kind of Caesarean operation, slits open the contracting walls and rescues his victim *in extremis.* . . .

In his life, Poe, who passed for the adorer of woman, thanks to his verse and ardent utterances was, in the depths of his soul, always flung back from his ecstatic attraction to-wards them to libidinal subjection to the male and, against this, the male in him constantly rebelled. The chaste and tender husband of the dying Virginia would leave her bed-side for sudden and, at times, long drinking "fugues" with bosom cronies. More significant still, Poe, paranoiac and persecuted, as usually happens, remained attached to his persecutors and, oddly, wished always to renew his friend-ship with them. His lamentable visit to Thomas Dunn En-glish to ask him to act as his second will be recalled, nor should we forget that it was his most treacherous and per-sistent enemy, Rufus Griswold, a man he had every reason to distrust, whom he desired to be his "executor"; a term one is tempted to take in its most literal sense!

Such, then, was the passivity retained by Poe, the adult, to father-figures: such was the mould he had acquired in child-hood under John Allan's roof, by contact with a rigid, pow-erful father whom he feared, hated, admired and, also, loved. . . . Poe's inveterate hatred of John Allan as, later, of all father-figures was, on a deeper level, a confession of indis-soluble attachment.

"Ligeia": Analyzing Poe's Love Stories

D.H. Lawrence

D.H. Lawrence is best known as the author of the controversial novels *Lady Chatterley's Lover, Women in Love,* and *Sons and Lovers.* In his work as well as in his life, Lawrence was obsessed with people's unconscious motives for their conscious actions, especially in male/female relationships. In this essay, originally published in Lawrence's critical collection *Studies in Classic American Literature,* Lawrence mines the same obsession as it relates to Poe's work. Reviewing Poe's story "Ligeia," Lawrence concludes that Poe was obsessed with becoming "one" with his female characters. Poe's unconscious motivations, Lawrence contemplates, may have marred his tales.

Poe had experienced the ecstasies of extreme spiritual love. And he wanted those ecstasies and nothing but those ecstasies. He wanted that great gratification, the sense of flowing, the sense of unison, the sense of heightening of life. He had experienced this gratification. He was told on every hand that this ecstasy of spiritual, nervous love was the greatest thing in life, was life itself. And he had tried it for himself, he knew that for him it *was* life itself. So he wanted it. And he *would have* it. He set up his will against the whole of the limitations of nature.

This is a brave man, acting on his own belief, and his own experience. But it is also an arrogant man, and a fool.

Poe was going to get the ecstasy and the heightening, cost what it might. He went on in a frenzy, as characteristic American women nowadays go on in a frenzy, after the very same thing: the heightening, the flow, the ecstasy. Poe tried alcohol, and any drug he could lay his hands on. He also tried any human being he could lay his hands on.

His grand attempt and achievement was with his wife; his cousin, a girl with a singing voice. With her he went in for the intensest flow, the heightening, the prismatic shades of ecstasy. It was the intensest nervous vibration of unison, pressed higher and higher in pitch, till the blood-vessels of the girl broke, and the blood began to flow out loose. It was love. If you call it love.

Love can be terribly obscene.

It is love that causes the neuroticism of the day. It is love that is the prime cause of tuberculosis.

The nerves that vibrate most intensely in spiritual unisons are the sympathetic ganglia of the breast, of the throat, and the hind brain. Drive this vibration over-intensely, and you weaken the sympathetic tissues of the chest—the lungs—or of the throat, or of the lower brain, and the tubercles are given a ripe field.

But Poe drove the vibrations beyond any human pitch of endurance.

Being his cousin, she was more easily keyed to him.

Ligeia is the chief story. Ligeia! A mental-derived name. To him the woman, his wife, was not Lucy. She was Ligeia. No doubt she even preferred it thus.

Ligeia is Poe's love-story, and its very fantasy makes it more truly his own story.

It is a tale of love pushed over a verge. And love pushed to extremes is a battle of wills between the lovers.

Love is become a battle of wills.

Which shall first destroy the other, of the lovers? Which can hold out longest, against the other?

Ligeia is still the old-fashioned woman. Her will is still to submit. She wills to submit to the vampire of her husband's consciousness. Even death.

"In stature she was tall, somewhat slender, and, in her latter days, even emaciated. I would in vain attempt to portray the majesty, the quiet ease, of her demeanour, or the incomprehensible lightness and elasticity of her footfall. . . . I was never made aware of her entrance into my closed study, save by the dear music of her low sweet voice, as she placed her marble hand upon my shoulder."

A MECHANICAL STYLE

Poe has been so praised for his style. But it seems to me a meretricious affair. "Her marble hand" and "the elasticity of her footfall" seem more like chair-springs and mantelpieces than a human creature. She never was quite a human creature to him. She was an instrument from which he got his extremes of sensation. His *machine à plaisir*, as somebody says.

All Poe's style, moreover, has this mechanical quality, as his poetry has a mechanical rhythm. He never sees anything in terms of life, almost always in terms of matter, jewels, marble, etc.,—or in terms of force, scientific. And his cadences are all managed mechanically. This is what is called "having a style."

What he wants to do with Ligeia is to analyse her, till he knows all her component parts, till he has got her all in his consciousness. She is some strange chemical salt which he must analyse out in the test-tubes of his brain, and then— when he's finished the analysis—*E finita la commedia!*

But she won't be quite analysed out. There is something, something he can't get. Writing of her eyes, he says: "They were, I must believe, far larger than the ordinary eyes of our own race"—as if anybody would want eyes "far larger" than other folks'. "They were even fuller than the fullest of the gazelle eyes of the tribe of the valley of Nourjahad"—which is blarney. "The hue of the orbs was the most brilliant of black and, far over them, hung jetty lashes of great length"— suggests a whiplash. "The brows, slightly irregular in outline, had the same tint. The 'strangeness,' however, which I found in the eyes, was of a nature distinct from the formation, or the colour, or the brilliancy of the features, and must, after all, be referred to the *expression.*"—Sounds like an anatomist anatomizing a cat—"Ah, word of no meaning! behind whose vast latitude of mere sound we entrench our ignorance of so much of the spiritual. The expression of the eyes of Ligeia! How for long hours have I pondered upon it! How have I, through the whole of a midsummer night, struggled to fathom it! What was it—that something more profound than the well of Democritus—which lay far within the pupils of my beloved! What *was* it? I was possessed with a passion to discover. . . ."

It is easy to see why each man kills the thing he loves. To *know* a living thing is to kill it. You have to kill a thing to know it satisfactorily. For this reason, the desirous consciousness, the SPIRIT, is a vampire.

One should be sufficiently intelligent and interested to

know a good deal *about* any person one comes into close contact with. *About* her. Or *about* him.

But to try to *know* any living being is to try to suck the life out of that being.

Above all things, with the woman one loves. Every sacred instinct teaches one that one must leave her unknown. You know your woman darkly, in the blood. To try to *know* her mentally is to try to kill her. Beware, oh woman, of the man who wants to *find out what you are.* And, oh men, beware a thousand times more of the woman who wants to *know* you, or *get* you, what you are.

It is the temptation of a vampire fiend, is this knowledge.

Man does so horribly want to master the secret of life and of individuality *with his mind.* It is like the analysis of protoplasm. You can only analyse *dead* protoplasm, and know its constituents. It is a death-process.

Keep KNOWLEDGE for the world of matter, force, and function. It has got nothing to do with being.

But Poe wanted to know—wanted to know what was the strangeness in the eyes of Ligeia. She might have told him it was horror at his probing, horror at being vamped by his consciousness.

But she wanted to be vamped. She wanted to be probed by his consciousness, to be KNOWN. She paid for wanting it, too.

Nowadays it is usually the man who wants to be vamped, to be KNOWN.

Edgar Allan probed and probed. So often he seemed on the verge. But she went over the verge of death before he came over the verge of knowledge. And it is always so.

He decided, therefore, that the clue to the strangeness lay in the mystery of will. "And the will therein lieth, which dieth not . . ."

Ligeia had a "gigantic volition." . . . "An intensity in thought, action, or speech was possibly, in her, a result, or at least an index" (he really meant indication) "of that gigantic volition which, during our long intercourse, failed to give other and more immediate evidence of its existence."

I should have thought her long submission to him was chief and ample "other evidence."

"Of all the women whom I have ever known, she, the outwardly calm, the ever-placid Ligeia, was the most violently a prey to the tumultuous vultures of stern passion. And of such passion I could form no estimate, save by the miraculous expansion of those eyes which at once so delighted and appalled me—by the almost magical melody, modulation, distinctness, and placidity of her very low voice—and by the fierce energy (rendered doubly effective by contrast with her manner of utterance) of the wild words which she habitually uttered."

Poor Poe, he had caught a bird of the same feather as himself. One of those terrible cravers, who crave the further sensation. Crave to madness or death. "Vultures of stern passion" indeed! Condors.

But having recognized that the clue was in her gigantic volition, he should have realized that the process of this loving, this craving, this knowing, was a struggle of wills. But Ligeia, true to the great tradition and mode of womanly love, by her will kept herself submissive, recipient. She is the passive body who is explored and analysed into death. And yet, at times, her great female will must have revolted. "Vultures of stern passion!" With a convulsion of desire she desired his further probing and exploring. To any lengths. But then, "tumultuous vultures of stern passion." She had to fight with herself.

But Ligeia wanted to go on and on with the craving, with the love, with the sensation, with the probing, with the knowing, on and on to the end.

OBSESSION

There is no end. There is only the rupture of death. That's where men, and women, are "had." Man is always sold, in his search for final KNOWLEDGE.

"That she loved me I should not have doubted; and I might have been easily aware that, in a bosom such as hers, love would have reigned no ordinary passion. But in death only was I fully impressed with the strength of her affection. For long hours, detaining my hand, would she pour out before me the overflowing of a heart whose more than passionate devotion amounted to idolatry." (Oh, the indecency of all this endless intimate talk!) "How had I deserved to be so blessed by such confessions?" (Another man would have felt himself cursed.) "How had I deserved to be so cursed with the removal of my beloved in the hour of her making them? But upon this subject I cannot bear to dilate. Let me say only that in Ligeia's more than womanly abandonment to a love, alas! all unmerited, all unworthily bestowed, I at length recognized the principle of her longing, with so wildly earnest a desire, for the life which was now fleeing so rapidly away. It is this wild longing—it is this eager vehemence of desire for life—*but* for life, that I have no power to portray, no utterance capable of expressing."

Well, that is ghastly enough, in all conscience.

"And from them that have not shall be taken away even that which they have."

"To him that hath life shall be given life, and from him that hath not life shall be taken away even that life which he hath."

Or her either.

These terribly conscious birds, like Poe and his Ligeia, deny the very life that is in them; they want to turn it all into talk, into *knowing.* And so life, which will *not* be known, leaves them.

But poor Ligeia, how could she help it? It was her doom. All the centuries of the spirit, all the years of American rebellion against the Holy Ghost, had done it to her.

She dies, when she would rather do anything than die. And when she dies the clue, which he only lived to grasp, dies with her.

Foiled!

Foiled!

No wonder she shrieks with her last breath.

On the last day Ligeia dictates to her husband a poem. As poems go, it is rather false, meretricious. But put yourself in Ligeia's place, and it is real enough, and ghastly beyond bearing.

> Out—out are all the lights—out all!
>   And over each quivering form
> The curtain, a funeral pall,
>   Comes down with the rush of a storm,
> While the angels, all pallid and wan,
>   Uprising, unveiling, affirm
> That the play is the tragedy, 'Man,'
>   And its hero, the Conqueror Worm.

Which is the American equivalent for a William Blake poem. For Blake, too, was one of these ghastly, obscene "Knowers."

"'O God!' half shrieked Ligeia, leaping to her feet and extending her arms aloft with a spasmodic movement, as I made an end of these lines—'O God! O Divine Father! shall these things be undeviatingly so? Shall this conqueror be not

once conquered? Are we not part and parcel in Thee? Who—
who knoweth the mysteries of the will with its vigour? Man
doth not yield him to the angels, *nor unto death utterly,* save
only through the weakness of his feeble will.'"
So Ligeia dies. And yields to death at least partly. *Anche
troppo.*
As for her cry to God—has not God said that those who
sin against the Holy Ghost shall not be forgiven?
And the Holy Ghost is within us. It is the thing that
prompts us to be real, not to push our own cravings too far,
not to submit to stunts and high-falutin, above all, not to be
too egoistic and wilful in our conscious self, but to change as
the spirit inside us bids us change, and leave off when it bids
us leave off, and laugh when we must laugh, particularly at
ourselves, for in deadly earnestness there is always something a bit ridiculous. The Holy Ghost bids us never be too
deadly in our earnestness, always to laugh in time, at ourselves and everything. Particularly at our sublimities. Everything has its hour of ridicule—everything.
Now Poe and Ligeia, alas, couldn't laugh. They were frenziedly earnest. And frenziedly they pushed on this vibration
of consciousness and unison in consciousness. They sinned
against the Holy Ghost that bids us all laugh and forget, bids
us know our own limits. And they weren't forgiven.
Ligeia needn't blame God. She had only her own will, her
"gigantic volition" to thank, lusting after more consciousness, more beastly KNOWING.
Ligeia dies. The husband goes to England, vulgarly buys
or rents a gloomy, grand old abbey, puts it into some sort of
repair, and furnishes it with exotic, mysterious, theatrical
splendour. Never anything open and real. This theatrical
"volition" of his. The bad taste of sensationalism.
Then he marries the fair-haired, blue-eyed Lady Rowena
Trevanion, of Tremaine. That is, she would be a sort of
Saxon-Cornish blue-blood damsel. Poor Poe!
"In halls such as these—in a bridal chamber such as this—
I passed, with the Lady of Tremaine, the unhallowed hours
of the first month of our marriage—passed them with but little disquietude. That my wife dreaded the fierce moodiness
of my temper—that she shunned me and loved me but little—
I could not help perceiving, but it gave me rather pleasure
than otherwise. I loathed her with a hatred belonging more
to demon than to man. My memory flew back (oh, with what

intensity of regret!) to Ligeia, the beloved, the august, the beautiful, the entombed. I revelled in recollections of her purity . . ." etc.

Now the vampire lust is consciously such.

In the second month of the marriage the Lady Rowena fell ill. It is the shadow of Ligeia hangs over her. It is the ghostly Ligeia who pours poison into Rowena's cup. It is the spirit of Ligeia, leagued with the spirit of the husband, that now lusts in the slow destruction of Rowena. The two vampires, dead wife and living husband.

For Ligeia has not yielded unto death *utterly*. Her fixed, frustrated will comes back in vindictiveness. She could not have her way in life. So she, too, will find victims in life. And the husband, all the time, only uses Rowena as a living body on which to wreak his vengeance for his being thwarted with Ligeia. Thwarted from the final KNOWING her.

And at last from the corpse of Rowena, Ligeia rises. Out of her death, through the door of a corpse they have destroyed between them, reappears Ligeia, still trying to have her will, to have more love and knowledge, the final gratification which is never final, with her husband.

For it is true, as William James and Conan Doyle and the rest allow, that a spirit can persist in the after-death. Persist by its own volition. But usually, the evil persistence of a thwarted will, returning for vengeance on life. Lemures, vampires.

It is a ghastly story of the assertion of the human will, the will-to-love and the will-to-consciousness, asserted against death itself. The pride of human conceit in KNOWLEDGE.

There are terrible spirits, ghosts, in the air of America. . . .

[Poe] was an adventurer into vaults and cellars and horrible underground passages of the human soul. He sounded the horror and the warning of his own doom.

Doomed he was. He died wanting more love, and love killed him. A ghastly disease, love. Poe telling us of his disease: trying even to make his disease fair and attractive. Even succeeding.

Which is the inevitable falseness, duplicity of art, American art in particular.

The Psychology of "The Tell-Tale Heart"

E. Arthur Robinson

In the following selection, Poe scholar E. Arthur
Robinson examines the psychological motivation
of the two main characters as well as certain elements in the story "The Tell-Tale Heart." Robinson
is especially fascinated by Poe's use of suspended
slow motion in the tale, how this technique influences the action of the two main characters and the
reader's response to the effect. He concludes that the
narrator's hatred for the old man in the tale is an
allegory for the loathing of self-discovery.

Poe's "The Tell-Tale Heart" consists of a monologue in
which an accused murderer protests his sanity rather than
his innocence. The point of view is the criminal's, but the
tone is ironic in that his protestation of sanity produces an
opposite effect upon the reader. From these two premises
stem multiple levels of action in the story. The criminal, for
example, appears obsessed with defending his physic self at
whatever cost, but actually his drive is self-destructive since
successful defense upon either implied charge—of murder
or of criminal insanity—automatically involves admission of
guilt upon the other.

Specifically the narrator bases his plea upon the assumption that madness is incompatible with systematic action,
and as evidence of his capacity for the latter he relates how
he has executed a horrible crime with rational precision. He
reiterates this argument until it falls into a pattern: "If still
you think me mad, you will think so no longer when I describe the wise precautions I took for concealment of the
body." At the same time he discloses a deep psychological
confusion. Almost casually he admits lack of normal motivation: "Object there was none. Passion there was none. I

Excerpted from "Poe's *The Tell-Tale Heart*" by E. Arthur Robinson. Copyright ©1965 by
The Regents of the University of California. Reprinted from *Nineteenth-Century Fiction*,
vol. 19, no. 4 (March 1965), pp. 369-78, by permission.

loved the old man." Yet in spite of this affection he says that the idea of murder "haunted me day and night." Since such processes of reasoning tend to convict the speaker of madness, it does not seem out of keeping that he is driven to confession by "hearing" reverberations of the still-beating heart in the corpse he has dismembered, nor that he appears unaware of the irrationalities in his defense of rationality.

At first reading, the elements of "The Tell-Tale Heart" appear simple: the story itself is one of Poe's shortest; it contains only two main characters, both unnamed, and three indistinguishable police officers; even the setting of the narration is left unspecified. In the present study my object is to show that beneath its narrative flow the story illustrates the elaboration of design which Poe customarily sought, and also that it contains two of the major psychological themes dramatized in his longer works.

It is important to note that Poe's theory of art emphasizes development almost equally with unity of effect. There must be, he insists, "a repetition of purpose," a "dropping of the water upon the rock;" thus he calls heavily upon the artist's craftsmanship to devise thematic modifications of the "preconceived effect." A favorite image in his stories is that of arabesque ornamentation with repetitive design. In "The Tell-Tale Heart" one can distinguish several such recurring devices filling out the "design" of the tale, the most evident being what the narrator calls his "over acuteness of the senses." He incorporates this physical keenness into his plea of sanity: "... why *will you* say that I am mad? The disease has sharpened my senses—not destroyed, not dulled them. Above all was the sense of hearing acute." He likens the sound of the old man's heart to the ticking of a watch "enveloped in cotton" and then fancies that its terrified beating may arouse the neighbors. His sensitivity to sight is equally disturbing, for it is the old man's eye, "a pale blue eye, with a film over it," which first vexed him and which he seeks to destroy. Similar though less extreme powers are ascribed to the old man. For example, the murderer congratulates himself that not even his victim could have detected anything wrong with the floor which has been replaced over the body, and earlier he imagines the old man, awakened by "the first slight noise," listening to determine whether the sound has come from an intruder or "the wind in the chimney." Variations such as these give the sensory details a thematic significance similar to that of the "morbid acuteness of the senses" of Roderick Usher in "The Fall of the House of Usher" or the intensity with which the victim of the Inquisition hears, sees, and smells his approaching doom in "The Pit and the Pendulum."

These sensory data provide the foundation for an interesting psychological phenomenon in the story. As the characters listen in the darkness, intervals of strained attention are prolonged until the effect resembles that of slow motion. Thus for seven nights the madman enters the room so "very, very slowly" that it takes him an hour to get his head through the doorway; as he says, "a watch's minute-hand moves more quickly than did mine." When on the eighth night the old man is alarmed, "for a whole hour I did not move a muscle." Later he is roused to fury by the man's terror, but "even yet," he declares, "I refrained and kept still. I scarcely breathed." On different nights both men sit paralyzed in bed, listening for terrors real or imagined. After the murder is completed, "I placed my hand upon the heart and held it there many minutes." In the end it seems to his overstrained nerves that the police officers linger inordinately in the house, chatting and smiling, until he is driven frantic by their cheerful persistence.

THE ARCHITECTURAL PRINCIPLE

This psychological process is important to "The Tell-Tale Heart" in two ways. First, reduplication of the device gives the story structural power. Poe here repeats a dominating impression at least seven times in a brief story. Several of the instances mentioned pertain to plot, but others function to emphasize the former and to provide aesthetic satisfaction. To use Poe's words, "by such means, with such care and skill, a picture is at length painted which leaves in the mind of him who contemplates it with a kindred art, a sense of the fullest satisfaction. The idea of the tale, its thesis, has been presented unblemished. . . ." Here Poe is speaking specifically of "skilfully-constructed tales," and the complementary aspects of technique described are first to omit extraneous material and second to combine incidents, tone, and style to develop the "pre-established design." In this manner, form and "idea" become one. The thematic repetition and variation of incident in "The Tell-Tale Heart" offer one of the clearest examples of this architectural principle of Poe's at work.

Second, this slow-motion technique intensifies the subjectivity of "The Tell-Tale Heart" beyond that attained by mere use of a narrator. In the psychological triad of stimulus, internal response, and action, the first and third elements are slighted and the middle stage is given exaggerated attention. In "The Tell-Tale Heart," stimulus in an objective sense scarcely exists at all. Only the man's eye motivates the murderer, and that almost wholly through his internal reaction to it. The action too, though decisive, is quickly over: "In an instant I dragged him to the floor, and pulled the heavy bed over him." In contrast, the intermediate, subjective experience is prolonged to a point where psychologically it is beyond objective measurement. At first the intervals receive conventional description—an "hour," or "many minutes"—but eventually such designations become meaningless and duration can be presented only in terms of the experience itself. Thus, in the conclusion of the story, the ringing in the madman's ears first is "fancied," then later becomes "distinct," then is discovered to be so "definite" that it is erroneously accorded external actuality, and finally grows to such obsessive proportions that it drives the criminal into an emotional and physical frenzy. Of the objective duration of these stages no information is given; the experience simply "continued" until "at length" the narrator "found" that its quality had changed.

Through such psychological handling of time Poe achieves in several of his most effective stories, including "The Tell-Tale Heart," two levels of chronological development which are at work simultaneously throughout the story. Typically, the action reaches its most intense point when the relation between the objective and subjective time sense falters or tails. At this point too the mental world of the subject is at its greatest danger of collapse. Thus we have the mental agony of the bound prisoner who loses all count of time as he alternately swoons and lives intensified existence while he observes the slowly descending pendulum. The narrator in "The Pit and the Pendulum" specifically refuses to accept responsibility for objective time-correlations: "There was another interval of insensibility; it was brief; for, upon again lapsing into life, there had been no perceptible descent in the pendulum. But it might have been long; for I knew there were demons who took note of my swoon, and who could have arrested the vibration at pleasure." These demons are his Inquisitional persecutors, but more subjective "demons" are at work in the timeless terror and fascination of the mariner whirled around the abyss in "The Descent into the Maelström," or the powerless waiting of Usher for days after he first hears his sister stirring within the tomb. In each instance the objective world has been reduced to the microcosm of an individual's experience; his time sense fades under the pressure of emotional stress and physical paralysis.

A SYMBOLIC PARALYSIS

Even when not literally present, paralysis often may be regarded as symbolic in Poe's stories. In *The Narrative of Arthur Gordon Pym* (1838), Pym's terrifying dreams in the hold of the ship represent physical and mental paralysis: "Had a thousand lives hung upon the movement of a limb or the utterance of a syllable, I could have neither stirred nor spoken. . . . I felt that my powers of body and mind were fast leaving me." Other examples are the "convolutions" of bonds about the narrator in "The Pit and the Pendulum," the death-grasp on the ring-bolt in "The Descent into the Maelstrom," the inaction of Roderick and (more literally) the catalepsy of Madeline Usher, and in part the supposed rationality of the madman in "The Tell-Tale Heart," which turns out to be subservience of his mental to his emotional nature. In most applications of the slow-motion technique in "The Tell-Tale Heart," three states of being are present concurrently: emotional tension, loss of mental grasp upon the actualities of the situation, and inability to act or to act deliberately. Often these conditions both invite and postpone catastrophe, with the effect of focusing attention upon the intervening experience.

In the two years following publication of "The Tell-Tale Heart," Poe extended this timeless paralysis to fantasies of hypnosis lasting beyond death. "Mesmeric Revelation" (1844) contains speculations about the relation between sensory experience and eternity. In "The Facts in the Case of M. Valdemar" (1845) the hypnotized subject is maintained for nearly seven months in a state of suspended "death" and undergoes instant dissolution when revived. His pleading for either life or death suggests that his internal condition had included awareness and suffering. Similarly the narrator in "The Tell-Tale Heart" records: "Oh God! what *could* I do? I foamed—I raved—I swore!" while all the time the police officers notice no foaming nor raving, for still they "chatted pleasantly, and smiled." His reaction is still essentially subjective, although he paces the room and grates his chair upon the boards above the beating heart. All these experiences move toward ultimate collapse which is reached in "The Tell-Tale Heart" as it is for Usher and the hypnotized victims, while a last-moment reprieve is granted in "The Pit and the Pendulum" and "The Descent into the Maelström."

A second major theme in "The Tell-Tale Heart" is the murderer's psychological identification with the man he kills. Similar sensory details connect the two men. The vulture eye which the subject casts upon the narrator is duplicated in the "single dim ray" of the lantern that falls upon his own eye; like the unshuttered lantern, it is always one eye that is mentioned, never two. One man hears the creaking of the lantern hinge, the other the slipping of a finger upon the fastening. Both lie awake at midnight "hearkening to the death-watches in the wall." The loud yell of the murderer is echoed in the old man's shriek, which the narrator, as though with increasing clairvoyance, later tells the police was his own. Most of all the identity is implied in the key psychological occurrence in the story—the madman's mistaking his own heartbeat for that of his victim, both before and after the murder.

SLOW-MOTION TECHNIQUE

These two psychological themes—the indefinite extension of subjective time and the psychic merging of killer and killed—are linked closely together in the story. This is illustrated in the narrator's commentary after he has awakened the old man by an incautious sound and each waits for the other to move:

> Presently I heard a slight groan, and I knew it was the groan of mortal terror. It was not a groan of pain or of grief—oh, no!—it was the low stifled sound that arises from the bottom of the soul when overcharged with awe. I knew the sound well. Many a night, just at midnight, when all of the world slept, it has welled up from my own bosom, deepening, with its dreadful echo, the terrors that distracted me. I say I knew it well. I knew that he had been lying awake ever since the first slight noise, when he had turned in the bed. His fears had been ever since growing upon him. He had been trying to fancy them causeless, but could not. He had been saying to himself—"Is it nothing but the wind in the chimney—it is only a mouse crossing the floor," or "it is merely a cricket

which has made a single chirp." Yes, he had been trying to comfort himself with these suppositions: but he had found all in vain.

Here the slow-motion technique is applied to both characters, with emphasis upon first their subjective experience and second the essential identity of that experience. The madman feels compelled to delay the murder until his subject is overcome by the same nameless fears that have possessed his own soul. The groan is an "echo" of these terrors within. The speaker has attempted a kind of catharsis by forcing his own inner horror to arise in his companion and then feeding his self-pity upon it. This pity cannot prevent the murder, which is a further attempt at exorcism. The final two sentences of the paragraph quoted explain why he believes that destruction is inevitable:

> *All in vain*; because Death, in approaching him, had stalked with his black shadow before him, and enveloped the victim. And it was the mournful influence of the unperceived shadow that caused him to feel—although he neither saw nor heard—*to feel* the presence of my head within the room.

The significance of these sentences becomes clearer when we consider how strikingly the over-all effect of time-extension in "The Tell-Tale Heart" resembles that produced in Poe's "The Colloquy of Monos and Una," published two years earlier. In Monos's account of dying and passing into eternity, he prefaces his final experience with a sensory acuteness similar to that experienced by the narrator in "The Tell-Tale Heart." "The senses were unusually active," Monos reports, "though eccentrically so. . . ." As the five senses fade in death, they are not utterly lost but merge into a sixth—of simple duration:

> Motion in the animal frame had fully ceased. No muscle quivered; no nerve thrilled; no artery throbbed. But there seems to have sprung up in the brain . . . a mental pendulous pulsation. . . . By its aid I measured the irregularities of the clock upon the mantel, and of the watches of the attendants. . . . And this—this keen, perfect, self-existing sentiment of *duration* . . . this sixth sense, upspringing from the ashes of the rest, was the first obvious and certain step of the intemporal soul upon the threshold of the temporal Eternity.

Likewise the old man in "The Tell-Tale Heart" listens as though paralyzed, unable either to move or to hear anything that will dissolve his fears. This resembles Monos' sensory intensity and the cessation of "motion in the animal frame."

Also subjective time is prolonged, becomes partially divorced from objective measurement, and dominates it. The most significant similarity comes in the conclusion of the experience. The old man does not know it but he is undergoing the same dissolution as Monos. He waits in vain for his fear to subside because actually it is "Death" whose shadow is approaching him, and "it was the mournful influence of that shadow that caused him to feel" his destroyer within the room. Like Monos, beyond his normal senses he has arrived at a "sixth sense," which is at first duration and then death.

But if the old man is nearing death so too must be the narrator, who has felt the same "mortal terror" in his own bosom. This similarity serves to unify the story. In Poe's tales, extreme sensitivity of the senses usually signalizes approaching death, as in the case of Monos and of Roderick Usher. This "over acuteness" in "The Tell-Tale Heart," however, pertains chiefly to the murderer, while death comes to the man with the "vulture eye." By making the narrator dramatize his feelings in the old man, Poe draws these two motifs together. We must remember, writes one commentator upon the story, "that the criminal sought his own death in that of his victim, and that he had in effect become the man who now lies dead." Symbolically this is true. The resurgence of the beating heart shows that the horrors within himself, which the criminal attempted to identify with the old man and thus destroy, still live. In the death of the old man he sought to kill a part of himself, but his "demons" could not be exorcised through murder, for he himself is their destined victim.

From this point of view, the theme of "The Tell-Tale Heart" is self-destruction through extreme subjectivity marked paradoxically by both an excess of sensitivity and temporal solipsism. How seriously Poe could take this relativity of time and experience is evident in the poetic philosophy of his *Eureka* (1849). There time is extended almost infinitely into the life-cycle of the universe, but that cycle itself is only one heartbeat of God, who is the ultimate subjectivity. Romantically, indeed, Poe goes even further in the conclusion to *Eureka* and sees individual man becoming God, enclosing reality within himself, and acting as his own creative agent. In this state, distinction between subjective and objective fades: "the sense of individual identity will be gradually merged in the general consciousness." Destruction then becomes self-destruction, the madman and his victim being aspects of the same universal identity. Death not only is self-willed but takes on some of the sanctity of creative and hence destructive Deity. The heartbeat of the red slayer and the slain merge in Poe's metaphysical speculations as well as in the denouement of a horror story.

An Unresolved Ending

This extreme subjectivity, moreover, leaves the ethical problem of "The Tell-Tale Heart" unresolved. In the opening paragraph of the story is foreshadowed an issue of good and evil connected with the speaker's madness: "I heard all things in the heaven and in the earth. I heard many things in hell. How, then, am I mad?" To be dramatically functional such an issue must be related to the murder. The only outward motivation for the murder is irritation at "the vulture eye." It is the evil of the eye, not the old man (whom he "loved"), that the murderer can no longer live with, and to make sure that it is destroyed he will not kill the man while he is sleeping. What the "Evil Eye" represents that it so arouses the madman we do not know, but since he sees himself in his companion the result is self-knowledge. Vision becomes insight, the "Evil Eye" an evil "I," and the murdered man a victim sacrificed to a self-constituted deity. In this story, we have undeveloped hints of the self-abhorrence uncovered in "William Wilson" and "The Imp of the Perverse."

Poe also has left unresolved the story's ultimate degree of subjectivity. No objective setting is provided; so completely subjective is the narration that few or no points of alignment with the external world remain. From internal evidence, we assume the speaker to be mad, but whether his words constitute a defense before some criminal tribunal or the complete fantasy of a madman there is no way of ascertaining. The difference, however, is not material, for the subjective experience, however come by, *is* the story. Psychologically, the lengthening concentration upon internal states of being has divorced the murderer first from normal chronology and finally from relationship with the "actual" world. The result, in Beach's words, is "disintegration of the psychological complex." The victim images himself as another and recoils from the vision. Seeing and seen eye become identical and must be destroyed.

"The Fall of the House of Usher": An Allegory of the Artist

Daniel Hoffman

Daniel Hoffman, Poet in Residence and Felix E. Schelling Professor of English Emeritus at the University of Pennsylvania, was the 1973–74 Consultant in Poetry of the Library of Congress, the appointment now designated Poet Laureate. He is author of *Form and Fable in American Fiction, The Poetry of Stephen Crane* and other books. While a Research Fellow of the American Council of Learned Societies, Hoffman began his work on Poe, entitled *Poe, Poe, Poe, Poe, Poe, Poe, Poe*, from which this article is excerpted. Hoffman defines what he believes are Poe's themes in "The Fall of the House of Usher," including incest, murder, and madness. He concludes that the tale is an allegory about the artist and his creation.

Although written in 1839 . . . 'The Fall of the House of Usher' seems a thesaurus not only of Gothic clichés but also of nearly all of Poe's obsessional motifs; here joined together in a dazzling, garish, and intricately consistent pattern of concentric meanings. Because all tends toward the final annihilation, some critics have succumbed to the temptation to read the tale as a dramatization of *Eureka* [another Poe novel]. True, all of Poe's tales partake of the same fixities which he so bravely schematized there, yet I do not believe that any writer of successful fictions undertakes to tell a tale in order to demonstrate his theory of the cosmos. On the contrary, he more likely is driven by the imaginative pressure of his fictions to construct such a theory that will justify and explain them. . . .

In 'The Fall of the House of Usher' Poe completes what seems to me the tripartite division of functions in his most comprehensive and compelling tales. This is a fable of the soul: the soul acting independently, insofar as it can, insofar as it must, of mind, and struggling, as best it can, to be free, or, in the end, to become free, of the body.

Edgar Poe's *donnée* was nothing if not peculiar, yet its peculiarities are expressed in an inherited vocabulary of truisms. Body, Mind, and Soul: the functions defined by Greek philosophy, by the medieval scholastics. In his use of philosophical and psychological conceptions, as of literary conventions, Poe puts clichés to startling new uses. The result is almost always *weird*. Yet his characters and their catastrophes, strange though they be, despite the narrator's claim that he 'could not, even with effort, connect [Usher's] Arabesque expression with any idea of simple humanity,' do touch our own simple humanity. . . .

As is true of nearly all of Poe's Arabesques, the form of 'Usher' is that of a confessional monologue. . . . By means of this contrivance Poe is enabled to endow his most subjective fiction with an air of objectivity: this is not a madman's confession, but the report, by a sensible observer, of the dire predicament of someone else. . . .

[As Richard Wilbur maintains,] 'We must understand "The Fall of the House of Usher" as a dream of the narrator's, in which he leaves behind him the waking, physical world and journeys inward toward his *moi intérieur,* toward his inner and spiritual self. That inner and spiritual self is Roderick Usher.' Let me support this assertion by pointing out how Narrator and Usher are brought together in the tale. Narrator refers to Usher as 'one of my boon companions in boyhood' and to himself as Usher's 'best and indeed his only personal friend.' Nevertheless,

> Although, as boys, we had been even intimate associates, yet I really knew little of my friend. His reserve had always been excessive and habitual. I was aware, however, that his very ancient family had been noted, time out of mind, for a peculiar sensibility of temperament, displaying itself, through long ages, in many works of exalted art and manifested, of late, in repeated deeds of munificent yet unobtrusive charity.

THE NARRATOR

. . . To obey the summons of the boyhood friend who, in the subliminal allegory of this consistent plot represents his own unconscious, Narrator feels an overwhelming apprehension as he sees the House. Which is the House of Usher, the domain of his soul, into which he will be ushered. He feels this most keenly as he views its image, and the image of its zigzag flaw, in the dark tarn—as though Nature herself were offering an image like those proffered by art, as an exemplum of a truth more prophetic and more true than reality itself, which is apprehended only as an appearance.

Indeed, the appearance of the House, at its first glimpsing, is rendered by the narrator as though it were not an actual abode but a *picture of itself.* Brooding on the impossibility of analyzing his premonitions of woe, he says,

> It was possible, I reflected, that a mere different arrangement of the particulars of the scene, of the details of the picture, would be sufficient to modify, or perhaps to annihilate its capacity for sorrowful impression. . . .

But then he sees its 'inverted images' in the pool's reflection, and shudders yet again. So the reflection becomes the image of an image. And that image is described, with careful consistency, in terms of a human head: 'vacant and eye-like windows,' the 'web-like fungi' resembling Usher's 'hair of a more than web-like tenuity and softness.' Not surprisingly, the 'House of Usher' refers to 'both the family and the family mansion.' Once within the manse, Narrator is conducted 'through many dark and intricate passages,' reaching, at last, 'the *studio* of the master.' And this . . . is a chamber of crimsoned lights, of furniture, books, musical instruments in disorganized profusion. It is yet another symbol of the interior of a disordered mind. . . .

Madeline

Once Narrator has arrived he learns, as though for the first time, that this boon companion of his boyhood has a sister. He sees her only once—'While he spoke, the lady Madeline (for so she was called) passed through a remote portion of the apartment, and, without having noticed my presence, disappeared. I regarded her with an utter astonishment not unmingled with dread; and yet I found it impossible to account for such feelings.'

Does she really not notice his presence? For long, she has been sick, with an undiagnosed disease—'apathy . . . wasting away . . . a partially cataleptical character'—but no sooner does Narrator set foot in her house than 'she succumbed (as her brother told me at night with inexpressible agitation).' Now she lies dying; later, as Narrator and Roderick lay her out in the vault downstairs, Narrator notices 'a striking similitude' between Madeline and Roderick. Now, for the first time, the brother murmurs that they are twins 'and that sympathies of a scarcely intelligible nature had always existed between them.'. . .

No sooner does Madeline seem to be dying than Roderick becomes inconsolable, and he then commences—strangely— the only actions he instigates himself in this chronicle of the fall of his House. These actions are his artistic creations, for Roderick is a polymath of creative genius. The instruments which had lain disused upon the floor, the books scattered unattended in his studio, are suddenly put to use. Hitherto, Usher had been unmanned by his terrors—'I dread the events of the future, not in themselves, but in their results'; he was immobilized by a superstitious conviction that the House, from which he never ventured forth, held an influence over his spirit; and by the thought of 'the evidently approaching dissolution—of a tenderly beloved sister, his sole companion.' Now that Madeline at last is dying, what does Roderick do but burst forth with painted images, with song, with poetry!

Usher the painter is an artist of pure abstraction. 'If ever mortal painted an idea, that mortal was Roderick Usher.'

> A small picture presented the interior of an immensely long and rectangular vault or tunnel, with low walls, smooth, white, and without interruption or device . . . this excavation lay at an exceeding depth below the surface of the earth. No outlet was observed in any portion of its vast extent, and no torch or other artificial source of light was discernible; yet a flood of intense rays rolled throughout, and bathed the whole in a ghastly and inappropriate splendor.

MADELINE'S DEATH

. . . After some time spent in reading (Usher's 'chief delight' is the perusal of the rites for the dead), one night the host tells Narrator 'abruptly' that Madeline 'was no more.' With precipitate haste he plans to inter her in a vault downstairs. Narrator assists as Usher places his sister's body in this deep vault, which in feudal times had been used 'for the worst purposes' (doubtless as torture-chamber). It seems an image of the vault whose image formed the idea of Roderick Usher's eerie painting. At last Madeline is laid out, the lid of her coffin screwed down, and the heavy door grates into place.

This vault, lined with copper, deep in the bowels of the

House so interchangeable with its inmates, cannot help but suggest at-once a family tomb and an ancestral womb. In the event, Madeline is to rise again and reappear, as in a horrible travesty of rebirth. But we well know how strangely intercommunicable, for Poe, are images of suffering one's death and dying into life. No wonder the vault in Roderick's painting glowed with self-begotten light.

Now that Madeline is consigned there, Roderick's composure disintegrates. 'Some imaginary sound' afflicts him. There is in the air a terror which reason cannot dispel. Narrator, too, is affected by 'an incubus of utterly causeless alarm.'

Outside the House of Usher, Nature or supernature lends to the hysteria within the agitation of a whirlwind and the weird 'glowing in the unnatural light of a faintly luminous and distinctly visible gaseous exhalation which hung about and enshrouded the mansion.' Narrator dismisses these as 'merely electrical phenomena,' and to divert the terrified Roderick, commences to read aloud from one of his favorite romances, 'The Mad Trist' by Sir Launcelot Canning (an author invented by Poe). The passage he reads is

> that well-known portion of the story where Ethelred, the hero of the Trist, having sought in vain for peaceable admission into the dwelling of the hermit, proceeds to make good an entrance by force.

And here, in a style of 'uncouth and unimaginative prolixity' so little adapted to 'the lofty and spiritual ideality' of Usher, follows the action of Ethelred, advancing through the storm to bash down the door and slay the dragon, which expires with a horrible shriek. While Narrator is reading this, Roderick becomes transfixed; for with his hyper-acute ears he is hearing a door being burst apart and a howling shriek echoing up the stairs from the vault below. With a preternatural conjunction between the text of the romance and the actions of the avenging shade downstairs—a conjunction which imposes the armor of allegory upon the *dénouement* of the tale—while Ethelred is hacking his way in to the blessed place, Madeline is scratching her way *out* of her premature entombment. Yet the analogy is both obverse and exact, for, as will be seen, Madeline too is crossing the threshold of beatitude, escaping premature burial to enter the doorway, at last, of death, blessed death. . . .

With his supersensitive hearing Roderick has heard everything—heard her vain scratchings of the copper

sheaths, her feeble movements in the coffin, and now, inter-
mingled with the heroic actions of Ethelred, her bursting
from her coffin and thrusting apart the iron doors.

> Have I not heard her footstep on the stair? Do I not distin-
> guish that heavy and horrible beating of her heart?... *Mad-*
> *man! I tell you that she now stands without the door!*

...He cannot escape her vengeance now, as under 'the
potency of a spell,' the panels of the door swung open 'their
ponderous and ebony jaws.' There, with blood upon her
white robes, stood 'the lofty and enshrouded figure'... who,
'with a low moaning cry, fell heavily inward upon the person of her brother, and in her violent and now final death-
agonies, bore him to the floor a corpse, and a victim to the
terrors he had anticipated.'

An Allegory of the Unconscious

I must try to gather up some loose strands of this eerie web-
work. In the design of this fable, just as Roderick Usher is a
double of Narrator—unconsciousness as an emanation of
the conscious self—so is Madeline Usher the double of Roderick. Of these duplicate Ushers there is yet a further split,
for the House itself is both the Usher family and its manse,
as the bodily parallels and metaphors make plain.

Roderick, from the depths of a morbid depression brought
on by doubts of his sanity, has summoned Narrator to his remote House, riddled with intricate subterranean passages.
Of the lofty Madeline, Narrator, or consciousness, is, save for
Roderick's presence, wholly unaware. Now, enacting his desire to murder his beloved double, Usher inters her in a
vault from which she forcibly bursts free, as though in a
ghastly travesty of rebirth, in order to fall upon him, dead at
last. The House collapses inward upon its inmates as inorganic matter dissolves with organic.

Madeline is Usher's twin, his sister, his lover, and—but
this is true *only when he can think of her as dying*—his
muse. It is as though her dying is a precondition for the exercise of his creative impulse. The notion that the artwork
outlives its subject is indeed an old one, but Poe makes the
artist a cannibal or vampire whose subject *must die so* that
there may be art....

Not even the unconscious self can cope with such knowledge, for which there is no forgiveness. Once Roderick has
interred his sister beyond, as he thinks, hope of escape, his

'lofty reason . . . totters' and his creative spell is shattered. From this point comes the equivocal ending of 'The Haunted Palace' and his wild despairs. Unacknowledged guilt has broken him. Meantime, deep below in her sealed and cuprous vault, the body of his soul prepares to avenge herself by bursting forth to carry him with her into the final release of actual death.

HOUSE OF DREAD

This excerpt from "The Fall of the House of Usher" begins with the narrator's approaching Roderick's house, revealing Poe's use of symbolism: Roderick's house resembles a person.

I looked upon the scene before me—upon the mere house, and the simple landscape features of the domain—upon the bleak walls—upon the vacant eye-like windows—upon a few rank sedges—and upon a few white trunks of decayed trees— with an utter depression of soul which I can compare to no earthly sensation more properly than to the after-dream of the reveller upon opium—the bitter lapse into every-day life—the hideous dropping off of the veil. There was an iciness, a sinking, sickening of the heart—an unredeemed dreariness of thought which no goading of the imagination could torture into aught of the sublime. What was it—I paused to think— what was it that so unnerved me in the contemplation of the House of Usher? It was mystery all insoluble; nor could I grapple with the shadowy fancies that crowded upon me as I pondered. I was forced to fall back upon the unsatisfactory conclusion, that while, beyond doubt, there *are* combinations of very simple natural objects which have the power of thus affecting us, still the analysis of this power lies among considerations beyond our depth.

'The Fall of the House of Usher,' then, is both a testament to the autonomy of the unconscious, by whose inexorable powers are revealed the deepest truths of the soul, and, like 'Ligeia,' a fable of the one strange love story which was Poe's doom and gift. A love story in which incest, murder, and necrophilia are inescapable. To love one's twin sister is but a double displacement for the ultimate narcissism, self-love, and the ultimate incestuous desire, possession of one's mother's body. But in this strange domain from which all thought of ethics is banished as though by law—by an aesthetic law—there is yet, despite all, the sway of a moral law.

There is even here the invisible reign of that most ancient tabu, inspiring guilt and terror. In the archaic memory of the author, from which these terrible fantasies have risen, the image of the beloved is so inextricably enshrouded with the image of her death that his figure of the unconscious must doubly punish himself, imagining not only that his beloved twin and sister is dying or dead, but *making himself responsible* for her dissolution. His guilt is doubled, too, for not only does he become her murderer, he has done this terrible thing in order to make her 'lofty and enshrouded figure' the more completely correspond to his own desire. His erotic needs are subsumed in his art-products. His guitar rhapsodies, his poems, his paintings, all these can come into being only when his love-object exactly fits the imperious demands of his deepest wish. But that wish makes him the committer of both incest and murder, and his 'lofty reason' must topple from her throne. . . .

AN APOCALYPSE

I have but to underline the obvious source of Roderick Usher's self-immolating course of action: What caused him to put his sister living in the tomb? What but his inescapable Imp of the Perverse, willing his own destruction on the instant and through the mechanism of making him will hers. As she falls inward upon him, their House, whose zigzag fault may represent the inorganic impulse toward self-annihilation, falls inward upon them both, and the entire House of Usher, the living, the dead, and the unliving, sink beneath the primal waters of the tarn in a landslide like that of the City in the Sea. A total apocalypse, from which but one character—Narrator—escapes to tell the tale.

Narrator is usually taken to be a blockhead, for he seems stupid indeed to accept so unquestioningly so many strange doings in the household of his host. . . . Poe seems to me to be telling us that consciousness alone cannot understand the inexorable *donnée* of the unconscious, but also that the unconscious, if unaided by consciousness, is the victim of the very forces among which it dwells. Why else does Roderick at the outset *send for Narrator to join him*, but that Usher fears he is losing his reason? What Poe further tells us is, those forces which the unconscious knows but cannot control are so strong that the conscious mind, even when made aware of them, cannot do much to direct them either.

This latter inference is both borne out and belied by Narrator's tale, for what is the effect of his telling his tale but to control these very forces which, the tale says, overwhelm Roderick Usher? The tale begins by proposing that the harmonious collaboration of Narrator-plus-Usher, i.e. of the conscious *and* the unconscious, will have a therapeutic effect upon the latter in its extremity. By the end, we have, not, I think, 'catastrophe without tragedy,' but a *tale* of the personal apocalypse of the unconscious, as told by the conscious mind. Now it is true that Narrator is a bit dim, that in the eerie *monde intérieur* of Usher's House he functions with the insight of a Prefect of Police. But in his own house how does he function? He tells the tale in which we learn all this. I take that tale itself to be the result of the collaboration between the Narrator-portion and the Usher-meed of the author's own mind. It is the result of a harmonious collaboration between his conscious and unconscious mind.

Thus Narrator is both inside and outside the catastrophic events of which he speaks. By separating the body that dies from the soul that suffers and creates, and the suffering soul from the mind that ratiocinates, Poe has managed to escape the fate that overtakes Roderick Usher as a result of this same division of functions. For Poe, as Narrator, is outside the apocalypse, observing that in which he took a part as did God in Ligeia's poem 'The Conqueror Worm,' or in Poe's own *Eureka.*

Thus just as the several art-works within the tale are epitomes of the whole, so Roderick's action in creating them are epitomes of the author's in creating the tale of which they are among the parts. I speak now of Poe as author, no longer of Narrator, the character who tells the story, because I must rejoin those faculties in Poe which Poe has separated in Narrator and Usher: consciousness and intuition. These two qualities are exhibited in Roderick only while he functions as an artist. Before his creative streak which the presence of Narrator and Madeline's attendant sickness instigated, he was distraught. After reciting 'The Haunted Palace' he is overpowered by the 'evil things' the poem foretold—his own destructive impulses. Narrator, for his part, has no tale at all to tell save for the materials which his trip to Usher's domain had made available to him. Little though he consciously understands those experiences, in his telling of the tale we see the collaboration of Usher's intuitive power with Narrator's conscious mind. Like so many other of Poe's tale-tellers, his art-product transcends his own limitations to exhibit a design of which he is scarcely aware. The art-product which proceeds according to the principle of the economy of the means, and toward the predetermined end of exciting the beholder's soul, is *imputed to* Roderick Usher's improvisations. But it is enacted in the tale of the Fall of the House of Usher.

Creative intelligence, then, the fusion of intellect-cum-intuition, is, in the artist, the musician, the poet, a power which transcends the materials upon which it exercises its will and imposes its design. Like God, the artist is both embodied in and apart from the destruction of the creatures of his will. Like God, he outlives the annihilation of his self-created universe and can at will construct another plot containing yet again the necessity of its own destruction. Solipsism, in thought, in art, in life or death, can go no further than this. . . .

THE HERO AS ARTIST

The story offers Usher as a paradigm of the hero as artist, of the artist as *isolato,* of art as prophecy, of prophecy as burdened with doom. All this, though elaborated from Gothic clichés already tired by Poe's own time, strikes the thoughtful reader today as peculiarly modern. It is a form of our own anguish which is limned in these outlandish pages.

More generally, it is the grip this tale has upon the emotion of the uncanny which chills us. However repulsive one finds Poe's Gordian knot of incest, inhumation, murder and madness, his plot yet touches some unadmitted chord deep within us. It is akin to that almost forgotten knowledge toward which Poe's mariner rushed on his spectral ship, that nearly-recollected wisdom enshrined in Ligeia's eyes. Basing his investigation of 'the uncanny' upon an analysis of a tale by E.T.A. Hoffmann, whose work was among Poe's models, Freud proposed

> that we are able to postulate the principle of a *repetition-compulsion* in the unconscious mind, based upon instinctual activity and probably inherent in the very nature of the instincts—a principle powerful enough to overrule the pleasure-principle. . . . Whatever reminds us of this inner *repetition-compulsion* is perceived as uncanny.

Unusual as are Poe's particular obsessions and compulsions, the attachments of which they are vacant forms and the instincts which they embody are the common properties of our human inheritance. Thus Poe, out of the very peculiarity of his psychic makeup, speaks to us not as a psychotic but as a man. Few writers have lived with their unconscious pulsations so close to the surface of their skins. Few have been as able to summon these images, or been as unable to escape them, as was Edgar Poe.

CHRONOLOGY

1804

Meriwether Lewis and William Clark explore the northwestern United States.

1809

Edgar Allan Poe is born in Boston on January 19 to actors Elizabeth Arnold Poe and David Poe.

1811

David Poe deserts his family; Poe's mother dies in Richmond. Poe is taken in by John and Frances Allan and is christened Edgar Allan Poe.

1812

War of 1812 between Great Britain and United States begins.

1814

Napoléon exiled to Elba.

1815

Poe goes to England with Allans, attends Manor House School from 1817–1820.

1820

Poe returns to Richmond after Allan's business fails, attends Joseph Clarke's school, and later a school run by William Burke; national census: population 9,638,453; 7 percent urban, 93 percent rural; Missouri Compromise reached.

1823

President James Monroe issues Monroe Doctrine warning European powers not to interfere in Latin America.

1825

John Allan inherits large sum of money.

1826

Poe becomes engaged to Sarah Elmira Royster; enrolls at the

University of Virginia; leaves in December after having incurred gambling debts; becomes estranged from John Allan.

1827

Engagement with Elmira Royster broken; Royster goes on to marry A.B. Shelton; Poe runs away to Boston and enlists in army; publishes *Tamerlane and Other Poems.*

1829

Frances Allan dies, prompting a temporary reconciliation between John Allan and Poe; Poe requests and receives discharge from the army; *Al Aaraaf, Tamerlane, and Minor Poems* is published in Baltimore.

1830

Writes "To Helen"; enters West Point; John Allan remarries, severs relations with Poe.

1831

Expelled from West Point; goes to New York to live, then on to Baltimore; publishes *Poems;* Writes "Israfel" and *Tales of the Folio Club.*

1832

Publishes five tales, "Metzengerstein" being the most important.

1833

Wins a fifty-dollar prize from *Baltimore Saturday Visiter* for "MS. Found in a Bottle."

1834

John Allan dies March 27, leaving nothing to Poe; Andrew Jackson defeats John Quincy Adams for presidency; Factory Act in England forbids employment of children under nine in factories.

1835

Begins writing reviews for *Southern Literary Messenger* in Richmond; in December assumes editorship of same journal; publishes "Berenice," "Morella," and "Hans Pfaal"; secretly marries his thirteen-year-old cousin, Virginia Clemm.

1836

Publicly marries Virginia; Texas wins independence from Mexico.

1837

Resigns editorship of *Southern Literary Messenger;* moves to New York; writes *The Narrative of Arthur Gordon Pym.*

1838

The Narrative of Arthur Gordon Pym published; "Ligeia" appears after Poe moves to Philadelphia.

1839

Becomes editor of *Burton's Gentleman's Magazine; Tales of the Grotesque and Arabesque* published in December, containing "The Fall of the House of Usher."

1840

Leaves *Burton's;* releases his own plans for a journal, but fails to get support for the project.

1841

Becomes editor of *Graham's Magazine* in April; publishes "The Murders in the Rue Morgue" and "A Descent into the Maelstrom"; health and financial problems worsen.

1842

Leaves *Graham's;* writes "The Oval Portrait," "The Mystery of Marie Roget," and "The Masque of the Red Death"; publishes famous review of Hawthorne's *Twice-Told Tales.*

1843

"The Gold-Bug" receives a one-hundred-dollar prize from the Philadelphia *Dollar Newspaper;* publishes "The Pit and the Pendulum," "The Tell-Tale Heart," and "The Black Cat."

1844

Moves back to New York with Virginia and Maria Clemm; writes for *Sunday Times* and later New York *Evening Mirror;* writes "The Purloined Letter."

1845

"The Raven" published, gaining Poe widespread recognition; becomes editor of *Broadway Journal;* publishes *Tales* and *The Raven and Other Poems.*

1846–1848

Mexican-American War; *The Communist Manifesto* written by Karl Marx and Friedrich Engels.

1846

Broadway Journal fails financially; Poe moves to a cottage in

Fordham with his wife and Maria Clemm; publishes "The Cask of Amontillado" and "The Philosophy of Composition"; Irish potato famine at its worst.

1847

Virginia dies; publishes "The Domain of Arnheim" and "Ulalume."

1848

Engaged briefly to Sarah Helen Whitman; gives famous lecture "The Poetic Principle"; publishes *Eureka;* California gold rush begins.

1849

Publishes "For Annie," "Eldorado," "Annabel Lee," and "The Bells"; romances Mrs. Richmond and Mrs. Shelton (Sarah Elmira Royster); dies in a Baltimore hospital on October 7.

FOR FURTHER RESEARCH

ABOUT POE

Hervey Allen, *Israfel: The Life and Times of Edgar Allan Poe.* 2 vols. New York: Rinehart, 1949.

William Bittner, *Poe: A Biography.* New York: Little Brown, 1962.

John Evangelist, *Plumes in the Dust: The Love Affair of Edgar Allan Poe and Sarah Osgood.* Chicago: Nelson Hall, 1980.

James A. Harrison, ed., *The Life and Letters of Edgar Allan Poe.* New York: Thomas Y. Crowell, 1902.

Robert D. Jacobs, *Poe: Journalist and Critic.* Baton Rouge: Louisiana State University Press, 1969.

Bettina L. Knapp, *Edgar Allan Poe.* New York: Ungar, 1984.

Joseph Wood Krutch, *Edgar Allan Poe: A Study in Genius.* New York: Russell and Russell, 1965.

Philip Lindsay, *The Haunted Man: A Portrait of Edgar Allan Poe.* New York: Philosophical Library, 1954.

Jeffrey Meyers, *Edgar Allan Poe: His Life and Legacy.* New York: Charles Scribner's Sons, 1992.

Sidney P. Moss, *Poe's Literary Battles.* Carbondale: Southern Illinois University Press, 1969.

John Ward Ostrom, ed., *The Letters of Edgar Allan Poe.* New York: Gordian Press, 1966.

Edd Winfield Parks, *Edgar Allan Poe as a Literary Critic.* Athens: University of Georgia Press, 1964.

Elizabeth Phillips, *Edgar Allan Poe: An American Imagination.* Port Washington, NY: Kennikat Press, 1979.

Arthur Hobson Quinn, *Edgar Allan Poe: A Critical Biography.* New York: Appleton/Century, 1941.

David Sinclair, *Edgar Allan Poe*. London: J.M. Dent & Sons, 1977.

Phillip Van Doren Stern, *Edgar Allan Poe: Visitor from the Night of Time*. New York: Cromwell, 1973.

Julian Symons, *The Tell-Tale Heart: The Life and Works of Edgar Allan Poe*. New York: Harper & Row, 1978.

Frances Winwar, *The Haunted Palace: A Life of Edgar Allan Poe*. New York: Harper, 1959.

Edgar Woodberry, *The Life of Edgar Allan Poe: Personal and Literary*. New York: Biblio and Tannen, 1965.

CRITICAL WORKS

Charles Baudelaire, *Selected Critical Studies of Baudelaire*. Cambridge, England: University Press, 1949.

Clive Bloom, *Reading Poe, Reading Freud: The Romantic Imagination in Crisis*. New York: St. Martin's, 1988.

Louis Broussard, *The Measure of Poe*. Norman: University of Oklahoma Press, 1969.

Vincent Buranelli, *Edgar Allan Poe*. Boston: G.K. Hall, 1977.

Eric W. Carlson, ed., *Critical Essays on Edgar Allan Poe*. Boston: G.K. Hall, 1987.

———, *Edgar Allan Poe: The Design of Order*. Totowa, NJ: Barnes and Noble, 1987.

———, *The Recognition of Edgar Allan Poe: Selected Criticism Since 1829*. Ann Arbor: University of Michigan Press, 1966.

John Phelps Fruit, *The Mind and Art of Poe's Poetry*. Folcroft, PA: Folcroft Library Editions, 1971.

Vernon W. Grant, *Great Abnormals: The Pathological Genius of Kafka, Van Gogh, Strindberg, and Poe*. New York: Hawthorne Books, 1968.

J.R. Hammond, *An Edgar Allan Poe Companion*. Totowa, NJ: Barnes and Noble, 1981.

James A. Harrison, ed., *The Complete Works of Edgar Allan Poe*. 17 vols. New York: Thomas Y. Crowell, 1902.

John T. Irwin, *The Mystery to a Solution: Poe, Borges, and the Analytic Detective Story*. Baltimore: Johns Hopkins University Press, 1994.

Arthur Lerner, *Psychoanalytically Oriented Criticism of Three American Poets: Poe, Whitman, Aiken.* Rutherford, NJ: Fairleigh Dickinson University Press, 1970.

Harry Levin, *The Power of Blackness: Hawthorne, Poe, Melville.* New York: Knopf, 1967.

John J. Moran, *A Defense of Edgar Allan Poe.* Washington, DC: William F. Boogher, 1885.

Burton R. Pollin, *Discoveries in Poe.* Notre Dame, IN: University of Notre Dame, 1970.

———, *Ruined Eden of the Present: Hawthorne, Melville, and Poe.* West Lafayette, IN: Purdue University Press, 1981.

David Punter, *The Literature of Terror: A History of Gothic Fictions from 1765 to the Present Day.* London: Longman, 1980.

Robert Regan, ed., *Poe: A Collection of Critical Essays.* Englewood Cliffs, NJ: Prentice-Hall, 1967.

Gary Thompson, *Poe's Fiction: Romantic Irony in Gothic Tales.* Madison: University of Wisconsin Press, 1973.

ABOUT POE'S TIME

James Stevens Curl, *The Victorian Celebration of Death.* Devon, England: David & Charles, 1972.

Daniel Walker Howe, *Victorian America.* Philadelphia: University of Pennsylvania Press, 1976.

Perry Miller, *The Raven and the Whale: The War of Words and Wits in the Era of Poe and Melville.* New York: Harcourt, Brace, 1956.

John Morley, *Death, Heaven, and the Victorians.* Pittsburgh: University of Pittsburgh Press, 1971.

John R. Reed, *Victorian Conventions.* Athens: Ohio University Press, 1975.

Lawrence Stone, *The Family, Sex, and Marriage in England, 1500–1800.* New York: Harper and Row, 1977.

INDEX

AIDS, 55, 56
"Al Aaraaf," 95, 115, 129, 132
Al Aaraaf, Tamerlane and Minor Poems, 20
Allan, Frances (foster mother of Poe), 16, 20
Allan, John (foster father of Poe), 16, 19-20, 151
and anger with Poe, 17, 18, 21
allegory. *See* characters; *Fall of the House of Usher, The*; symbolism
"Annabel Lee," 34, 54, 93, 94
Aristidean, 79
Assignation, The, 113-14, 116, 124
Astrov, Vladimir, 97
Auden, W.H., 57

Balloon Hoax, The, 25, 26
Baltimore, Md., 20, 21, 30
Baltimore Saturday Visitor, 21
Balzac, Honoré de, 46
Basler, Roy, 96
Baudelaire, Charles, 36, 41, 48, 63, 80
on Poe's genius, 32
"Bells, The," 28, 36, 57, 61
Benitez, R. Michael, 30
Berenice, 21, 95, 101-102, 127
Bible, the, 132, 133
Birkhead, Edith, 104
Bisco, John, 26
Black Cat, The, 22, 25, 85, 127
Blackwood's Magazine, 106
Blake, William, 157
Bonaparte, Marie, 148
Bon Bon, 21
Bonfire of the Vanities (Wolfe), 55
Booth, Edwin, 74
Boston, Mass., 15, 18, 50
Boston Nation, 23
Briggs, Charles, 26
Broadway Journal, 26, 106
Brownell, W.C., 73
Browning, Elizabeth Barrett, 73
Burduck, Michael L., 101
Burke, Edmund, 102, 104, 107

on pain/pleasure, 108
Burke, William, 16
Burton's Gentleman's Magazine, 23, 106
Byron, George, 38, 66

Cambiaire, Celestin Pierre, 44
Case of M. Valdemar, The, 125
Cask of Amontillado, The, 13, 27, 58
Castle of Otranto, The (Walpole), 103
Chandler, Frank W., 46
characters, Poe's, 51-53, 101, 129, 170
as allegorical figures, 82-83, 111-12, 116-18
autobiographical nature of, 35, 71, 156, 157
as caricatures, 121
and lack of learning, 130-31
passivity of, 59
and sensory data, 162
"City in the Sea," 36, 129, 176
Clarke, Joseph, 16-17
Clemm, Maria, 20, 21, 23, 28, 30
Colloquy of Monos and Una, The, 129, 166, 167
"Conqueror Worm, The," 36, 95, 100, 157, 177
Conversation of Eiros and Charmion, 129, 133
Cooke, Philip Pendleton, 101-102

Danse Macabre (King), 101
Dante Alighieri, 80
Davidson, Edward H., 18, 128
Delacroix, Eugène, 34-35
Depken, F., 47
Descent into the Maelström, A, 59, 83, 164, 165
Diamond as Big as the Ritz, The (Fitzgerald), 50
Dickens, Charles, 24, 25
Diderot, Denis, 33
Domain of Arnheim, The, 89

Dostoyevsky, Fyodor, 50, 60, 97
Doyle, Conan, 159
Duc de l'Omelette, The, 21, 113
"Eldorado," 28
Eleonora, 71-72, 89, 90
Eliot, T.S., 70, 80, 126
Elk, The, 89
English, Thomas Dunn, 79, 151
Eureka, 57, 87, 88, 169, 177
  philosophy in, 72, 133, 135, 167
  publication of, 27-28
  violates Poe's own literary theory,
    61-62

Fagin, N. Bryllion, 14, 64
Fall of the House of Usher, The, 13,
  85-86, 89, 123, 128
  as allegory of artist, 169
  as allegory of the unconscious,
    174-79
  as fable of the soul, 170
  Fitzgerald influenced by, 50, 51-
    53
  Madeline, 171-73, 174
  narrator, 170, 171, 176, 177
  popularity of, 23
  Roderick, 69, 111, 112, 129, 165
    acute senses of, 162, 173-74
    as artist, 172, 178
    refusal to face fear, 109
    resemblance to Poe, 71
    theme of fear in, 102, 109
    see also symbolism
Fitzgerald, F. Scott, 50-53
Fitzgerald, Zelda, 51
Foerster, Norman, 102
"For Annie," 28, 55
Forgotten Poet, A (Nabokov), 54
Four Beasts in One, 121, 122
France, 32, 46, 62
Fuller, Margaret, 73

Gilder, Jeannette L., 66
Godey's Lady's Book, 27
Goethe, Johann Wolfgang von, 42,
  80
Gold Bug, The, 25, 45, 54, 84
Gothic fiction. *See under* style
Graham, George, 23
Graham's Magazine, 23, 25, 26, 106
Griswold, Rufus, 13, 14, 25, 30, 151

Hallie, Philip P., 104
Haunted Palace, The, 36, 84, 86,
  175, 177
Hawthorne, Nathaniel, 24, 25, 49,
77, 78
Heller, Terry, 108
Hesiod, 62
History of Theatrical Art (Mantz-
  ius), 69
Histrionic Mr. Poe, The (Fagin), 14-
  15
Hoffman, Daniel, 169
Hood, Thomas, 38
Hop-Frog, 28, 113, 116, 122
Hopkins, Arthur, 70-71
Horton, W.T., 40
Hudson Review, 70
Hugo, Victor, 47
humor, 120-27
  and paradox, 126-27
  and physical degeneration, 124-
    26
  and satire, 122
  and self-revelation, 123
  see also style; themes
Hunter, William, 16
Huxley, Aldous, 36

Imp of the Perverse, The, 58, 168
Island of the Fay, The, 88

James, Henry, 66, 74, 126
James, William, 159
Jefferson, Thomas, 17
Justus, James H., 120

Kafka, Franz, 91
Keats, John, 65-66
Kennedy, J. Gerald, 92
Kennedy, John Pendleton, 67, 106
King, Stephen, 101-102

Landor Cottage, 89
language, 32, 41
  and metaphors, 124, 131
  and meter, 38, 39, 40, 144
    in "Ulalume," 37, 41-42, 61
  and proper names, 42-43, 120,
    153
  and tone, 141, 146
  and versification, 39, 41, 143
  see also style; symbolism
Lawrence, D.H., 59, 63, 109, 152
Lear, Edward, 43, 61
"Lenore," 93, 94
Letters of W.B. Yeats (Wade), 40
Ligeia, 22, 58, 62, 102, 123
  and descriptions of heroine, 154
  dreamlike quality of, 116
  and fascination with death, 96-
    100

as Poe's love story, 153
reflects Poe's search for knowl-
   edge, 155, 156, 157, 158
rooms in, 111, 113, 114
Rowena, 86, 96-100, 116, 158, 159
and will to live, 86, 95, 96
Lolita (Nabokov), 54-55
Longfellow, Henry Wadsworth, 78
Loss of Breath, 21, 124-25, 127
Lovecraft, H.P., 102, 107
Lucretius, 62

Mabbott, Thomas, 121, 124, 127
Mackenzie, William, 16
Mallarmé, Stéphane, 36, 63, 72, 80
Malone, Dumas, 69
Man of the Crowd, The, 58, 88
Man that Was Used Up, The, 23,
   124
Mantzius, Karl, 69
Marginalia, 107
Marvell, Andrew, 78
Maryland, 50, 51
Baltimore, 20, 21, 30
Masque of the Red Death, The, 25,
   55, 56, 88, 113
architectural allegory in, 117-18
Matthews, Brander, 44, 47
Maurice, Arthur Bartlett, 45
*Medical Inquiries and Observations
   upon the Diseases of the Mind*
   (Rush), 103
Melville, Herman, 49, 50, 53
Mémoires (Vidocq), 46, 47
Mesmeric Revelation, 87, 164
Metropolitan Museum of Fine Arts
   (New York), 74
Metzengerstein, 21, 86, 87
Meyers, Jeffrey, 21, 22, 27, 49
Milton, John, 26, 38, 39, 80
Moby-Dick (Melville), 49, 50
*Monsieur Dupin: The Detective Sto-
   ries of E.A. Poe*, 44, 45
Mooney, Stephen L., 87, 122
Moore, Thomas, 38
Morella, 21, 95, 96, 100, 102
has only Poe heroine who bears a
   child, 131
use of natural setting in, 89, 90
Mosses from an Old Manse (Haw-
   thorne), 25
MS. Found in a Bottle, 21, 83, 84,
   110
Murders in the Rue Morgue, The,
   23, 44, 45, 115
Mystery of Marie Roget, The, 25, 45

Nabokov, Vladimir, 53-55
Narrative of Arthur Gordon Pym,
   22, 49, 50, 59, 149
as adventure story, 59-60
influence on Melville, 53
as Poe's most important work, 57,
   84
symbolic paralysis in, 164
Nation magazine, 34
Nelson, Lowry, 103
New York Evening Mirror, 25
New York Sun, 26
Notes About Men of Note (English),
   79

Osgood, Frances (Fanny) Sargent,
   26, 27
Oval Portrait, The, 89, 113

Parks, Edd Winfield, 75
Parks, Richard Henry, 74
Parrington, Vernon Louis, 72
Penn (failed magazine of Poe's), 23
Philadelphia Saturday Courier, 21,
   23
Philosophy of Composition, 39-40,
   61, 80, 93
Philosophy of Furniture, The, 113
Pit and the Pendulum, The, 57, 134,
   163, 164
Freudian interpretation of, 148-51
and human imprisonment, 83
and loss of identity/conscious-
   ness, 84
nightmare quality of, 114
use of physical details in, 40
Poe, David (father), 15, 16
Poe, Edgar Allan, 137
army career of, 19, 20
childhood of, 66
education of, 16-18, 67
family of, 15, 50
final days of, 28-30, 159
genius of, 32-35
and self-creation, 71-72
and uniqueness, 178-79
letters of, 67-68
as literary critic, 25, 75-80
conflict caused by, 79
and defender of magazines, 75
on Hawthorne, 77
literary influences of, 13, 43, 60,
   161
on detective fiction, 44-46
on Fitzgerald, 50-53
on French writers, 46-47
on Lear, 61

on Melville, 49-50, 53
on modern literature, 91
on Nabokov, 53-55
on storytelling and poetry, 64,
    65
on Wolfe, 55-56
monument to, 74
personality of, 62-63, 64, 66
and reputation, 49, 56
and strong desires, 152, 155, 156
and theory of art, 76, 78, 80, 82,
    131
on poetic motivation, 95, 99-100
strangeness of, 118-19
see also "Raven, The"
weakness for alcohol, 13, 51, 53,
    67, 152
and depression/irrationality, 21,
    22, 25, 26-27, 29
exacerbated by Virginia's
    death, 28
Poe, Eliza (mother), 15
Poe, Henry (brother), 16, 20
Poe, Rosalie (sister), 15, 16
Poe, Virginia Clemm (wife), 21, 22,
    23-24, 51, 153
fatal illness of, 27, 28, 151
Poetic Principle, The, 28, 29, 80
Poets and Poetry of America, The
    (Griswold), 25
Pound, Ezra, 56
Premature Burial, The, 25
Preston, James, 17
Purloined Letter, The, 25, 45, 58
Putnam, George, 26, 27-28

Quinn, Patrick, 49

"Raven, The," 61, 93, 128, 134
as explained by Poe, 39-40, 137-47
length of, 138-39
refrain of, 140-42, 144, 146
setting of, 144-45
fame and popularity of, 13, 26, 27,
    57
narrator of, 96, 100
Reynolds, Jeremiah, 49
Richmond, Annie, 28
Robertson, John W., 68
Robinson, E. Arthur, 160
Rush, Benjamin, 103

Sartain, John, 28, 29
Saturday Review of Literature, 69-
    70
Shanks, Edward, 64

Shaw, George Bernard, 34
Shelley, Percy Bysshe, 26, 65-66
Shelton, Elmira Royster, 17, 18, 29
Sheppard Lee, 120
Shew, Marie Louise, 28
Silence–a Fable, 54, 88, 129, 132-33
Smith, C. Alphonso, 45
Snodgrass, Joseph, 29-30
Some Words with a Mummy, 126
Southern Literary Messenger, 21,
    22, 78, 106, 107
Specimen Days (Whitman), 87
Spectacles, The, 121
Stevens, Wallace, 80
Stevenson, Robert Louis, 60, 71
style, Poe's, 33, 60-61, 131
architectural principle of, 162
classical nature of, 34
effect of personality on, 65, 66-67
Gothic characteristics of, 103,
    108, 124, 169
and use of terror, 92, 101, 104-
    105
immaturity of, 70
mechanical quality of, 153-54
and refrain, 140-42, 144, 146
and rhetoric, 52, 59
and Romanticism, 64, 69, 130
strangeness of, 170
and slow-motion technique, 164,
    165-67
theatricality of, 65, 68-69
vulgarity of, 36, 37, 40, 41
see also language; symbolism
Stylus, 28
Sue, Eugène, 47
Swinburne, Algernon Charles, 38
symbolism, 91, 92, 147, 161, 167
of buildings, 85, 112, 117, 175,
    176
and rooms, 111, 113-14, 144
and creation of imaginary world,
    82
and dream-states, 110-11, 114,
    116, 118
of enclosure motifs, 83-84, 111-
    12, 144, 149
in *Fall of the House of Usher*, 85-
    86, 87, 89
of lighting, 115-16, 145
in nature, 34-39, 88, 89
as reflection of human soul, 90
and raven, 141-42, 147
see also characters; style; themes
System of Dr. Tarr and Prof. Fether,
    116, 118, 122, 127

Tale of Jerusalem, A, 21, 123
Tale of the Ragged Mountains, A, 25
Tales of Ratiocination, 44, 45, 46, 48
Tales of the Folio Club, 21
Tales of the Grotesque and Arabesque, 23, 120
"Tamerlane," 128
Tamerlane and Other Poems, 19
Tate, Allen, 125
Technique of the Mystery Story, The (Wells), 45, 46
Tell-Tale Heart, The, 13, 25, 160-68
  and confusion of narrator, 160-61
  handling of time in, 162, 163, 166
  subjectivity of, 163, 164, 165, 169
  unresolved ending of, 168
themes, 33, 87
  adventure, 59, 60
  beauty, 32, 86, 139-40
  death, 88, 92, 123-24, 125, 156
    author's anxiety about, 150, 151
    and beautiful women, 15, 93-95, 98-100
    physical details of, 126
    and ritual, 132-33
    sensations associated with, 149, 166, 167
  fear, 101-103, 148, 162, 164, 167
    confrontation of, 105, 109
    popular appeal of, 106, 107-108
  horror, 33-34, 104-105, 126, 135
    and apocalypse, 129, 132, 133, 134
    as challenge to American Renaissance, 102-103
    as insight into Romantic consciousness, 130
    and plausibility, 148
    as world without choice/rationality, 128-29
  longing, 95
  love, 153, 156, 159
  myth linked to science, 133-34
  nature of man, 122, 134
  principle of unity, 76, 123, 124, 135
  psychic conflict, 86, 102-103, 119, 163-64

  and madness, 168
  and paralysis, 129, 164-65, 166
  and unconscious self, 84, 85, 174-79
  use of will, 58, 86, 153, 155, 158
  after death, 159
  see also humor; symbolism
Thompson, G.R., 127
Three Tales of Edgar Poe (Dostoyevsky), 97
"To Helen," 28, 36
"To One in Paradise," 94
Twice-Told Tales (Hawthorne), 25, 77

"Ulalume," 36, 54, 100
  language and meter in, 37, 41-42, 61
University of Virginia, 17, 18
Unparalleled Adventure of One Hans Pfaall, The, 21

Valéry, Paul, 36, 62, 80
Valley of the Many-Colored Grass, 90
Varma, Devendra P., 104, 105
Verne, Jules, 60
Vidocq, François-Eugène, 46, 47
Virginia (state), 16, 17, 18, 50
Voltaire, 47

Wade, Allan, 40
Walpole, Horace, 103
Weiss, Susan Archer, 71
Wells, Carolyn, 45, 46
Wells, H.G., 60
Westminster Review, The, 46
White, Thomas Willis, 21, 22, 106
Whitman, Sarah Helen, 28, 67, 68, 69, 74
Whitman, Walt, 58, 87
Wilbur, Richard, 110
William Wilson, 59, 71, 89, 111
Winters, Yvor, 66
Wremia, 97

Yeats, W.B., 40, 97

Zadig (Voltaire), 47
Zayed, Georges, 82